2025 Social Security

2025 SOCIAL Security COLA increase SIMPLIFIED

Unlocking The Impact Cost Of Living Adjustments On Social Security, Retirement, And Veteran Benefits

By
Daniel Lohr

Copyright @2024 Daniel Lohr

All rights reserved. No part of this publication may be reproduced, distributed, or transmitted in any form or by any means, including photocopying, recording, or other electronic or mechanical methods, without the prior written permission of the author, except in the case of brief quotations embodied in critical reviews and certain other noncommercial uses permitted by copyright law.

This book is a work of the author and has been written with the intention to educate and inspire. The views expressed herein are those of the author and do not necessarily reflect the views of the publisher.

Table of Contents

Introduction	3
Why This Book?	5
Part 1	8
Understanding Social Security COLA	8
Chapter 1	8
What is COLA and Why Does it Matter?	8
1.2 How is COLA Calculated?	11
1.3 COLA and Your Monthly Benefits: Real-World Examples	13
Chapter 2	16
Factors Influencing the 2025 COLA	16
2.2 Expert Predictions and Estimates	20
2.3 Historical COLA Trends: Lessons from the Past	23
Chapter 3	27
Inflation's Impact on Your Purchasing Power	27
3.2 The Role of Economic Growth in COLA Adjustments	31
3.3 Long-Term Outlook for Social Security and COLA	34
Part 2	38
Maximizing Your Social Security Benefits	38
Chapter 4	38
Understanding Your Full Retirement Age	38
4.2 Early vs. Late Claiming: Weighing the Options	41
Chapter 5	48
Earnings Limits and How They Affect Your Benefits	48
5.2 Strategies for Working While Receiving Social Security	52

5.3 Taxation of Social Security Benefits	56
Chapter 6	60
Integrating Social Security with Pensions and Retirement Savings	60
6.2 Maximizing Your Income Streams in Retirement	65
6.3 Creating a Diversified Retirement Portfolio	69
Part 3	**73**
Planning for a Secure Retirement	**73**
Chapter 7	73
Estimating Your Retirement Expenses	73
7.2 Building a Realistic Retirement Budget	77
7.3 Adjusting Your Budget for Inflation and COLA Changes	82
Chapter 8	86
Investment Options for Retirees	86
8.2 Balancing Risk and Return in Your Portfolio	91
8.3 Protecting Your Investments from Inflation	95
Chapter 9	100
Understanding Medicare and Supplemental Coverage	100
9.2 Estimating Healthcare Expenses in Retirement	105
9.3 Strategies for Managing Healthcare Costs	110
Part 4	**115**
Special Considerations for Veterans	**115**
Chapter 10	115
Social Security Benefits for Veterans	115
10.2 Coordinating Social Security with VA Benefits	119
10.3 Special Considerations for Disabled Veterans	124
Chapter 11	128
Types of Benefits Available for Families	128

    11.2 Eligibility and Application Process   132
    11.3 Planning for the Financial Security of Your Family   137

Part 5   **142**
Resources and Next Steps   **142**

  Chapter 12   142
  Online Resources and Tools for Social Security Planning   142
    12.2 Retirement Planning Calculators and Tools   146
    12.3 Finding Reputable Financial Advice Online   150
  Chapter 13   155
  Choosing a Qualified Financial Advisor   155
    13.2 Questions to Ask Your Advisor   160
    13.3 Working with a Financial Planner to Achieve Your Goals 165
  Chapter 14   170
  Staying Informed About Social Security Policy   170
    14.2 Making Your Voice Heard: Contacting Your Representatives   174
    14.3 Joining Organizations that Support Retirement Security 178
  Chapter 15   182
  Conclusion   182

Introduction

Imagine this: You're sitting on your porch, sipping a well-deserved cup of coffee, finally enjoying the retirement you've worked so hard for. But then a nagging worry creeps in. Will your Social Security checks keep up with the rising cost of groceries, gas, and those unexpected medical bills?

That, my friend, is where the mystery of the Social Security COLA – the Cost-of-Living Adjustment – comes into play. It's designed to be your financial safety net, ensuring your benefits aren't eaten away by inflation. But let's be honest; understanding how it works can feel like deciphering a secret code!

As a financial planner, I've sat across from countless individuals, their faces etched with concern as they try to make sense of their retirement finances. I remember Sarah, a retired teacher, who was convinced she wouldn't be able to afford her medications with the rising cost of healthcare. Or John, a veteran, who was unsure how the COLA would impact his benefits and his family's financial security.

These are the real-life worries that keep people up at night. And that's precisely why I wrote this book.

"2025 Social Security COLA Increase SIMPLIFIED" is your lifeline in the sometimes turbulent waters of retirement planning. It's your guide to understanding how this year's COLA – set at 2.5% – will affect your wallet and what you can do to maximize your benefits.

Consider me your friendly guide, cutting through the jargon and complexity, sharing insider tips and real-world examples to help you navigate this often-confusing landscape.

In this book, we'll embark on a journey together, exploring:
- **The ins and outs of COLA:** We'll explain how it is calculated, why it matters, and why it might not always be enough to keep up with rising prices.
- **Innovative claiming strategies:** Discover the optimal time to start your benefits to maximize your lifetime income.
- **Practical budgeting and investment tips:** Learn how to make your money last, even with inflation and uncertain COLA increases.
- **Special considerations for veterans:** We'll address the unique circumstances veterans face regarding Social Security and related benefits.

This book is more than just numbers and formulas. It's about empowering you with the knowledge and confidence to make informed decisions about your financial future.

So, grab another cup of coffee, settle into your favorite chair, and let's demystify the world of Social Security COLA together. Your journey to a secure and fulfilling retirement starts now!

2025 Social Security

Why This Book?

Let's face it: navigating the world of Social Security can feel like trying to solve a complex puzzle blindfolded. When it comes to understanding how the Cost-of-Living Adjustment (COLA) impacts your benefits, it's easy to get lost in a maze of jargon and confusing calculations.

As a Financial Planner, I've seen firsthand how this lack of understanding can lead to missed opportunities and unnecessary financial stress, especially for those approaching retirement.

People are often left with burning questions:
- Will my Social Security benefits be enough to cover my expenses?
- How will the 2025 COLA affect my monthly income?
- What strategies can I use to maximize my benefits and secure my financial future?

That's why I wrote this book.
"2025 Social Security COLA Increase SIMPLIFIED" is your clear, concise, and actionable guide to demystifying Social Security COLA and taking control of your retirement planning.

Here's what makes this book different:

- **It cuts through the complexity:** I've stripped away the jargon and technical terms, presenting the information in a way that's easy to understand, even if you have no financial background.
- **It focuses on the 2025 COLA:** You'll get the latest projections and analysis, helping you understand how this year's COLA will specifically impact your benefits.
- **It's packed with practical strategies:** You'll learn proven techniques to maximize your benefits, coordinate Social Security with other income sources, and plan for a secure retirement, even with inflation concerns.
- **It addresses your unique needs:** Whether you're approaching retirement, already receiving benefits, or a veteran seeking clarity, this book provides tailored guidance.

This book is your roadmap to navigating Social Security COLA and achieving your retirement goals.

In these pages, you'll discover:
- **The secrets behind COLA calculation:** Understand how it's determined and why it might not always keep up with rising costs.
- **Proven claiming strategies:** Learn the optimal time to start your benefits to maximize your lifetime income.

- **Expert tips for budgeting and investing:** Create a solid financial plan that accounts for inflation and COLA fluctuations.
- **Valuable resources and support:** Connect with helpful tools and organizations to further empower your retirement journey.

Don't leave your retirement security to chance. Empower yourself with the knowledge and confidence you need to make informed decisions and enjoy the retirement you deserve.

Get your "2025 Social Security COLA Increase SIMPLIFIED" copy today and unlock the secrets to a financially secure future!

Part 1
Understanding Social Security COLA

Chapter 1
What is COLA and Why Does it Matter?

Think of Social Security as a financial safety net, something you've paid into throughout your working years, a promise that you'll have some income to rely on when you retire. But here's the thing: living costs, no, living costs, even everything from milk and bread to that new pair of shoes you've been eyeing, tend to creep up over time. That's called inflation, and it's a sneaky thief, quietly eroding the buying power of your hard-earned money.

Imagine if your Social Security checks stayed the same while prices kept climbing. Suddenly, that fixed income doesn't stretch as far. You might have to make tough choices, like cutting back on groceries or forgoing that annual trip to see the grandkids. That's where COLA swoops in to save the day!

COLA stands for Cost-of-Living Adjustment. It's a yearly increase to your Social Security benefits designed to help your payments keep pace with inflation. Think of it as a built-in raise, a way to help you maintain your standard of living even as prices rise.

You might wonder, "How much of a raise are we talking about?" That's where things get more interesting. The COLA isn't just a random number pulled out of a hat. It's carefully calculated based on the Consumer Price Index for Urban Wage Earners and Clerical Workers (CPI-W). Sounds like a mouthful. Sorry, I'll break it down. The CPI-W tracks the average price change paid by urban consumers for a basket of goods and services, such as food, housing, transportation, and medical care. It measures how much more (or less) it costs to live from one year to the next.

The Social Security Administration (SSA) uses this CPI-W data to determine the COLA for each year. For 2025, the COLA is set at 2.5%. That means if you received $1,500 per month in Social Security benefits in 2024, your payments would increase by $37.50 per month in 2025, bringing your total to $1,537.50.

2.5% might not sound like a huge jump, but even small increases can make a significant difference over time. Let's say you live another 20 years after retirement. That seemingly small COLA could add up to thousands of dollars in extra income over those years, helping you maintain your financial independence and enjoy your golden years without worrying about rising costs.

But here's the reality: COLA isn't always a perfect solution. Sometimes, inflation can be an actual card, jumping unexpectedly like a startled cat. In those cases, even the COLA might not be enough to offset the rising cost of living fully. That's why it's so important to understand how COLA works, how it affects your benefits, and what other steps you can take to protect your retirement savings from inflation's sneaky grasp.

Think of COLA as one piece of the retirement puzzle. It's a vital piece, but it's not the whole picture. By understanding COLA, planning your finances wisely, and staying informed about economic trends, you can take control of your financial future and enjoy the retirement you've worked so hard to achieve.

In the next section, we'll explore the factors that influence the COLA and what experts predict for the years to come. Stay tuned because knowledge is power, especially when it comes to securing your financial well-being in retirement!

1.2 How is COLA Calculated?

Remember that CPI-W we talked about earlier? The Consumer Price Index for Urban Wage Earners and Clerical Workers? That's the star of our show when it comes to calculating COLA. Think of it as a giant shopping cart filled with all the things people typically buy – groceries, gas, rent, doctor visits, you name it. The CPI-W tracks how the prices of those items change over time.

Here's where the math comes in, but don't worry—it's not rocket science. To calculate COLA, the Social Security Administration (SSA) looks at the CPI-W for the third quarter (July, August, September) of the current year. It compares it to the CPI-W for the third quarter of the previous year.

Let's say, for example, that the average CPI-W in the third quarter of 2024 was 300, and in the third quarter of 2023, it was 291.

To find the percentage change, we'd do a little subtraction and division:
- **Step 1: Find the difference:** 300 (2024) - 291 (2023) = 9
- **Step 2: Divide by the old number:** 9 / 291 = 0.031 (approximately)
- **Step 3: Multiply by 100 to get a percentage:** 0.031 x 100 = 3.1%

So, in this example, the CPI-W increased by 3.1%. That means the average cost of goods and services went up by that much. And that's how the SSA would arrive at the COLA for 2025.

Now, I know what you might be thinking: "But wait, the 2025 COLA is 2.5%, not 3.1%!" You're absolutely right! While the CPI-W is the primary factor in determining COLA, it's not the *only* factor.

The SSA also considers other economic data, like wage growth, to ensure the COLA accurately reflects the real-life financial pressures faced by Social Security beneficiaries. Sometimes, these additional factors can lead to a slight adjustment in the final COLA percentage.

It's also important to remember that the CPI-W is an average. It reflects the overall price changes for a broad range of goods and services. But your spending habits might differ from the average. For example, if you spend a more significant portion of your income on healthcare, which tends to have higher inflation rates, you might feel the pinch of rising costs even more with the COLA increase.

Now, let's talk about some common misconceptions about COLA. I've heard folks say things like, "COLA is just a government handout!" or "It's not enough to keep up with real inflation!"

Well, let's set the record straight. COLA is not a handout. It's a crucial part of the Social Security system, designed to protect the benefits you've earned throughout your working life. And while it's true that COLA might not always perfectly match every individual's cost of living increases, it plays a vital role in helping seniors maintain their financial security.

Think of it this way: Imagine you're on a sailboat in a choppy sea. The COLA is like the anchor that keeps you from drifting too far off course. It provides stability and helps you weather the storms of inflation.

In the next section, we'll examine the economic forces that influence COLA, including inflation, economic growth, and the long-term outlook for Social Security. So, grab your life jacket, and let's navigate these waters together!

1.3 COLA and Your Monthly Benefits: Real-World Examples

Imagine you're Mary, a recently retired librarian who loves spending her days tending to her rose garden and catching up with her grandkids. Mary receives $1,800 per month in Social Security benefits. Now, with the 2025 COLA set at 2.5%, her monthly check will get a little boost.

Here's how it works:

- **Calculate the increase:** $1,800 x 0.025 (2.5% as a decimal) = $45
- **Add the increase to the original amount:** $1,800 + $45 = $1,845

So, starting in January 2025, Mary will receive $1,845 per month, an increase of $45 thanks to the COLA. Now, $45 might not seem like a life-changing amount, but let's consider how that extra money can make a difference in Mary's life.

It may help her cover the rising cost of her prescription medications, allowing her to stay healthy and active. It may mean she can afford that new gardening tool she's been eyeing, bringing more joy to her favorite hobby. Or it provides a little extra cushion in her budget, giving her peace of mind knowing she can handle unexpected expenses without dipping into her savings.

Now, let's meet David, a retired construction worker who enjoys spending his retirement traveling and exploring new hobbies. David receives $2,200 per month in Social Security benefits.

With the 2025 COLA, his monthly check will also see a bump:
- **Calculate the increase:** $2,200 x 0.025 = $55
- **Add the increase to the original amount:** $2,200 + $55 = $2,255

David's extra $55 per month might allow him to afford that weekend getaway he's been planning or cover the increasing cost of his photography classes. It's all about maintaining his lifestyle and pursuing his passions in retirement.

Now, I know what you might be thinking: "These are just small examples. How does COLA really impact people's lives in the long run?"

Well, let's consider the bigger picture. Imagine Mary and David continue to receive their adjusted benefits for the next 15 years. Over that time, Mary's COLA increases would total over $8,100, while David's would total over $10,000!

That's a significant amount of money that can make a real difference in their ability to maintain their independence, cover their expenses, and enjoy their retirement years. It's the difference between feeling financially secure and constantly worrying about making ends meet.

But here's another critical point: COLA's impact isn't just about individual beneficiaries. It has ripple effects throughout the economy. When millions of seniors receive a COLA increase, they have more money to spend, which can boost local businesses, create jobs, and stimulate economic growth.

Think of it this way: When Mary has a little extra cash, she might treat herself to dinner at her favorite local restaurant, supporting the restaurant owner and their employees. David might use his COLA increase to buy a new camera from a local shop, helping that business thrive.

So, while COLA might seem like a personal financial matter, it's actually a vital part of a larger economic ecosystem. It's a win-win situation, providing financial security for seniors while also contributing to a healthy economy.

Now, I know what you're thinking: "This all sounds great, but what if the COLA doesn't keep up with my actual expenses?" That's a valid concern, and we'll address it in the next chapter when we dive deeper into the relationship between COLA, inflation, and the economy.

But for now, remember this: COLA is a powerful tool that can help you maintain your financial footing in retirement. It's a testament to the importance of Social Security and its role in ensuring a secure future for millions of Americans.

Chapter 2
Factors Influencing the 2025 COLA

Let's put on our detective hats and investigate the forces behind the 2025 COLA. It's like a financial whodunit, and we're about to uncover the clues that determine how much your Social Security checks will increase next year.

As we've learned, the Consumer Price Index for Urban Wage Earners and Clerical Workers (CPI-W) is the main character in our COLA story. But it's not a lone wolf. A whole cast of economic factors influences how much those prices rise (or fall), and that's what ultimately shapes the COLA.

Think of it like this: Imagine the CPI-W as a bustling marketplace, with vendors selling everything from apples and bread to gasoline and movie tickets. The prices in this marketplace are constantly changing and influenced by a complex web of forces.

One major player is **inflation**. It's like a mischievous gremlin that sneaks into the marketplace and starts raising prices. Inflation can be caused by various things, like increased demand for goods and services, supply chain disruptions (think about those cargo ships stuck in canals!), or even government policies.

When inflation is high, those prices in our CPI-W marketplace start climbing faster. And that, my friend, puts upward pressure on the

COLA. The SSA wants to ensure your benefits keep pace with those rising costs, so a higher inflation rate generally leads to a more significant COLA bump.

But inflation isn't the only force at play. Another key player is **economic growth**. When the economy is humming along nicely, businesses expand, people get jobs, and wages rise. That can also push prices up, as people have more money to spend and demand for goods and services increases.

Now, you might be thinking, "Wait a minute, doesn't economic growth mean things are good? Why would that lead to a higher COLA?" It's a balancing act. A strong economy is generally a good thing, but it can also lead to some inflation. The COLA is designed to help you stay afloat during those times of economic change, ensuring your benefits don't lose their purchasing power.

But here's where things get even more intricate. Sometimes, the economy can throw us a curveball. We might experience **stagflation**, a situation where inflation is high, but economic growth is sluggish. That can be a real head-scratcher for economists and policymakers. It's like the marketplace is getting more expensive, but people aren't necessarily better off.

In these situations, determining the COLA becomes even more challenging. The SSA has to weigh the impact of inflation on beneficiaries against the overall economic conditions. It's a delicate balancing act, and sometimes, the COLA might not fully capture the real-life financial pressures faced by seniors.

Another factor that can influence COLA is **government policy**. Decisions about taxes, spending, and interest rates can all have ripple effects on the economy and inflation. For example, if the government decides to print more money, that can lead to higher inflation, which could, in turn, push the COLA higher.

Let's not forget about global events. War, natural disasters, or even political instability in other countries can disrupt supply chains, affect energy prices, and ultimately influence the cost of goods and services here at home. These events remind us that our economy is interconnected with the rest of the world, and they can have a tangible impact on your pocketbook.

Now, I know what you might be thinking: "This is getting complicated!" And you're right, it is. But that's why it's so important to have a basic understanding of these economic forces. It helps you make sense of the COLA, anticipate potential changes, and plan your finances accordingly.

Think of it like this: You wouldn't set sail on a long voyage without understanding the winds and currents that might affect your journey. Similarly, understanding the economic factors that influence COLA is like having a nautical chart for your retirement finances. It helps you steer your course and reach your destination safely.

In the next section, we'll examine the predictions and projections for the 2025 COLA, exploring what experts say and what you can expect for your benefits next year. So, grab your compass, and let's continue our exploration!

2.2 Expert Predictions and Estimates

Think of it this way: Imagine you're planning a road trip. You wouldn't just hop in the car and start driving without checking the weather forecast, assessing traffic conditions, and getting some recommendations from seasoned travelers.

Similarly, when it comes to your Social Security benefits, it's wise to consult the experts, those who spend their days analyzing economic trends and crunching numbers. They can provide valuable insights and help you prepare for what's ahead.

Now, who are these experts, you ask? Well, they come from various backgrounds: economists, policy analysts, Social Security specialists, and even financial planners like myself. They use their knowledge and experience to make educated guesses about the future direction of the economy and how it might impact the COLA.

One key organization that monitors COLA closely is The Senior Citizens League (TSCL). This non-profit group advocates for the interests of older Americans and releases its own COLA projections based on the latest inflation data every month. As of October 2024, TSCL predicts that the 2025 COLA will be around 2.5%.

Now, it's important to remember that these are just projections. The actual COLA might be higher or lower depending on how the economy performs in the coming months. However, these estimates give us a good starting point and help us understand the range of possibilities.

Another group that weighs in on COLA is the Committee for a Responsible Federal Budget (CRFB). This nonpartisan organization focuses on fiscal policy. It analyzes Social Security's long-term sustainability and provides insights into how economic factors might affect the program's future, including COLA adjustments.

The CRFB often emphasizes the importance of controlling COLA to ensure Social Security's long-term solvency. They point out that if COLA increases are consistently higher than the actual increase in the cost of living for seniors, it could strain the program's finances.

Now, let's not forget about the financial gurus out there, those who make a living analyzing market trends and advising investors. Many financial publications, like Kiplinger and The Motley Fool, offer their own COLA predictions based on their economic outlook.

These predictions often take into account factors like energy prices, housing costs, and healthcare inflation, which can significantly impact seniors' budgets. They might also consider the Federal Reserve's monetary policy and its potential to influence inflation.

Of course, as a financial planner myself, I also monitor COLA projections closely. I use this information to help my clients plan their retirement income and make informed decisions about their Social Security benefits.

For example, if the projections suggest a lower-than-expected COLA, I suggest that my clients adjust their budgets, explore ways to supplement their income, or consider delaying their Social Security claims to maximize their benefits.

Now, I know what you might be thinking: "Why are there so many different predictions? Can't they just give us a straight answer?" Well, the truth is, predicting the future is a tricky business, especially when it comes to the economy.

Think of it like trying to predict the weather. Even the most sophisticated meteorologists, with all their fancy technology, can't always get it right. There are just too many variables at play.

Similarly, economic forecasts are based on a complex set of assumptions and data analysis. Different experts might use different models or weigh certain factors more heavily than others, leading to variations in their predictions.

But here's the good news: Even with these variations, expert predictions provide a valuable range of possibilities. They help us understand the potential impact of economic forces on our Social Security benefits and allow us to plan for different scenarios.

It's like having a map with multiple routes to your destination. You might encounter detours or unexpected roadblocks along the way, but having those alternative routes gives you flexibility and peace of mind.

In the next section, we'll take a step back and look at the bigger picture, exploring how historical COLA trends can provide valuable lessons for the future. So, buckle up, and let's continue our journey through the fascinating world of Social Security!

2.3 Historical COLA Trends: Lessons from the Past

Now, I know what you might be thinking: "History? Isn't that boring?" But trust me, looking at past COLA trends is like peeking into a financial rearview mirror. It helps us understand where we've been, where we might be going, and how to navigate the road ahead.

Think of it like this: Imagine you're learning to bake a cake. You wouldn't just throw ingredients together randomly, would you? You should look at a recipe, learn from experienced bakers, and try different techniques to see what works best.

Similarly, when it comes to understanding COLA, looking at historical trends is like studying a recipe for financial security in retirement. It shows us how COLA has responded to different economic conditions, how it has impacted beneficiaries, and what lessons we can learn from the past.

So, let's rewind the clock and take a quick tour through some critical moments in COLA history:

- **The Early Years (1975-1982):** COLA was a relatively new concept that was introduced in 1975. These were years of high inflation, and COLA increases were substantial, sometimes reaching double digits! Imagine getting a 14.3% raise in your benefits, like seniors did in 1980. That's enough to make a real difference in your budget!
- **The Calm Before the Storm (1983-2000):** Inflation calmed down in the 80s and 90s, and COLA increases became more moderate, typically ranging from 2% to 5%. This period showed that COLA could effectively keep pace with gradual price increases, providing a stable source of income for retirees.
- **The Rollercoaster Ride (2001-2020):** The early 2000s brought a mix of economic ups and downs, including the dot-com bubble burst and the Great Recession. COLA increases fluctuated accordingly, with some years seeing larger bumps (5.8% in 2009) and others seeing more minor adjustments or no increase (0% in 2010, 2011, and 2016). That period highlighted the volatility of economic conditions and their impact on COLA.
- **The Pandemic and Beyond (2021-Present):** The COVID-19 pandemic threw the global economy into a tailspin, causing

supply chain disruptions, labor shortages, and a surge in demand for certain goods. That led to a sharp spike in inflation, resulting in the highest COLA increase in decades – a whopping 8.7% in 2023! This unprecedented increase underscored the importance of COLA in protecting seniors' purchasing power during times of economic uncertainty.

Now, what can we learn from this historical rollercoaster? Well, a few key takeaways emerge:

- **COLA is not always predictable:** As we've seen, COLA can vary significantly from year to year, depending on economic conditions. It's not a guarantee of a specific percentage increase, and it's essential to be prepared for fluctuations.
- **Inflation is a key driver:** High inflation tends to lead to more significant COLA increases, while low inflation can result in more minor adjustments or even no increase. Keeping an eye on inflation trends can help you anticipate potential changes in your benefits.
- **COLA is essential for maintaining purchasing power:** Even during periods of moderate inflation, COLA plays a crucial role in ensuring that your benefits don't lose their value over time. It's a vital safeguard against the erosion of your retirement income.

- **Economic events can have a significant impact.** From recessions to pandemics, unexpected events can disrupt the economy and influence COLA. That is a reminder that retirement planning requires flexibility and adaptability.

Now, you might wonder: "How can I use this historical knowledge to plan for my retirement?" That's a great question!

Here are a few practical tips:
- **Don't rely solely on COLA:** While COLA is an integral part of your retirement income, it's not the only factor to consider. Diversify your income sources, build a substantial nest egg, and explore other strategies to protect your finances from inflation.
- **Stay informed about economic trends:** Monitor inflation reports, financial forecasts, and expert predictions. That will help you anticipate potential changes in COLA and adjust your plans accordingly.
- **Be prepared for unexpected events:** Life throws curveballs, and the economy is no exception. Build flexibility into your retirement plan so you can adapt to changing circumstances.
- **Don't panic over short-term fluctuations:** COLA might go up or down from year to year, but focus on the long-term trend. Social Security is designed to provide a stable source of income

throughout your retirement, and COLA plays a crucial role in that stability.

By learning from the past, staying informed about the present, and planning for the future, you can confidently navigate the twists and turns of retirement. Remember, knowledge is power, and understanding COLA is critical to securing your financial well-being in your golden years.

Chapter 3
Inflation's Impact on Your Purchasing Power

Let's talk about inflation, but in a way that feels less like an economics textbook and more like a real-life story. Because inflation isn't just some abstract concept—it's a sneaky villain that can quietly chip away at your retirement dreams if you're not careful.

Imagine this: you're strolling down memory lane, reminiscing about the "good old days" when a gallon of gas costs a dollar (or maybe even less!). A movie ticket was a few bucks, and you could buy a whole week's worth of groceries for what seems like a pittance today.

But then you snap back to reality, and those nostalgic memories are met with the harsh truth of today's prices. Suddenly, filling up your gas tank feels like a significant expense, and that trip to the grocery store leaves your wallet feeling significantly lighter.

That, my friend, is the power of inflation. It's the gradual increase in the prices of goods and services over time, a phenomenon that can silently erode the purchasing power of your hard-earned money.

Now, you might be thinking, "What does this have to do with my retirement?" Well, imagine you've diligently saved for your golden years, picturing yourself traveling the world, pursuing new hobbies, and enjoying a comfortable lifestyle. But if inflation isn't factored into your plans, those dreams could slowly fade away.

Let's say you've saved $500,000 for retirement, and you expect to live another 20 years. That might seem like a comfortable nest egg. Still, if inflation averages 3% per year (which is a historically moderate rate), the purchasing power of your savings will significantly decrease over time.

In fact, after 20 years, that $500,000 will have the same buying power as roughly $276,000 today. That means you'll effectively have lost almost half of your savings to inflation!

This erosion of purchasing power can have a tangible impact on your retirement lifestyle. That dream vacation might become less affordable, those weekly dinners might turn into monthly treats, and unexpected expenses could throw your budget into disarray.

Now, I know what you might be thinking: "But wait, isn't that what COLA is for? To protect my Social Security benefits from inflation?" You're absolutely right! COLA is a crucial tool in the fight against inflation, but it's not a magic bullet.

As discussed, COLA is based on the CPI-W, which measures the average price changes for a basket of goods and services. But your spending habits might differ from that average. For example, if you spend a significant portion of your income on healthcare, which tends to have higher inflation rates than other goods, you might feel the pinch of rising costs even more, even with the COLA increase.

Moreover, COLA is designed to protect your Social Security benefits, not your entire retirement savings. That's why it's crucial to have a comprehensive retirement plan that takes inflation into account and includes strategies to protect your nest egg from its erosive effects.

Think of it like this: Imagine you're building a house. COLA is like the foundation, providing a stable base for your retirement income. But you also need strong walls, a sturdy roof, and a storm shelter to protect your home from the elements.

Similarly, retirement planning requires a multi-faceted approach to safeguard your finances from inflation. This might include:

- **Diversifying your investments:** Don't put all your eggs in one basket. Spread your savings across different asset classes, like stocks, bonds, and real estate, to reduce risk and potentially outpace inflation.
- **Considering inflation-protected securities:** These are particular types of bonds that adjust their principal based on inflation, providing a guaranteed return that keeps pace with rising prices.

- **Investing in your health:** Staying healthy can help you reduce healthcare costs in retirement, which are often a significant source of inflation.
- **Downsizing or relocating:** If your housing costs are a significant burden, consider downsizing to a smaller home or relocating to a more affordable area.
- **Staying informed about economic trends:** Monitor inflation reports, financial forecasts, and expert predictions. That will help you anticipate potential challenges and adjust your plans accordingly.

By understanding the impact of inflation and taking proactive steps to protect your finances, you can build a secure and fulfilling retirement, even in the face of rising costs. It's about being proactive, informed, and adaptable so you can enjoy your golden years without constantly worrying about the shrinking value of your hard-earned savings.

3.2 The Role of Economic Growth in COLA Adjustments

Now, I know "economic growth" might sound like something better suited for a stuffy boardroom meeting, but trust me, it has a real impact on your retirement life.

Think of the economy as a giant engine that drives our society. When that engine is running smoothly, businesses thrive, jobs are created, and people have more money to spend. This increased spending creates demand for goods and services, which can lead businesses to raise their prices. Sounds familiar? Yes, it's that inflation gremlin we talked about earlier, but this time, it's got a slightly different costume.

Now, you might think, "Wait a minute, isn't economic growth good? Why would that lead to higher prices and potentially a smaller COLA?" Well, it's a balancing act. A strong economy is generally positive, leading to higher employment, increased wages, and a better standard of living for many. But it can also bring some inflationary pressure.

Imagine a popular restaurant in a bustling city. As more people have money to spend, the restaurant gets busier, and demand for its delicious meals increases. To keep up with the market and manage costs, the restaurant owner might decide to raise prices. It's a natural response to a thriving economy.

Similarly, when the economy grows, businesses across various sectors raise their prices to reflect increased demand and rising production costs. This overall increase in prices is what we call inflation.

Now, here's where COLA comes into play. Remember, COLA is designed to help your Social Security benefits keep pace with inflation. So, when the economy is growing, and inflation is ticking upward, the

COLA is likely to be higher to help you maintain your purchasing power.

But here's where things get interesting. The relationship between economic growth and COLA isn't always straightforward. Sometimes, the economy can grow without causing a significant surge in inflation. That is often referred to as "Goldilocks" growth—not too hot, not too cold, but just right.

In these scenarios, the COLA might be more moderate, even though the economy is doing well. The SSA takes a balanced approach, considering not just inflation but also other economic factors, like wage growth and productivity, to ensure the COLA accurately reflects seniors' financial reality.

Now, let's flip the coin and consider what happens when economic growth slows down. Imagine our bustling city suddenly experiencing a downturn. Businesses might struggle, jobs could be lost, and people might tighten their belts, spending less. This decreased demand can lead to lower inflation or even deflation in some cases.

In these situations, the COLA might be smaller, or in extreme cases, there might be no COLA increase at all. That happened in 2010, 2011, and 2016, during the aftermath of the Great Recession, when the economy was sluggish and inflation was low.

Now, is economic growth good or bad for my COLA? Well, it's not that simple. A healthy economy is generally beneficial for everyone, including Social Security beneficiaries. It means more jobs, higher wages, and a more substantial tax base to support Social Security.

But it's important to remember that economic growth can also bring inflationary pressures, which can impact the COLA. The key is to find a balance – an economy that grows steadily without causing runaway inflation.

Think of it like Goldilocks and porridge. We don't want the economy to be too hot (high inflation) or too cold (slow growth). We want it to be just right, with sustainable development that supports a healthy COLA and protects your retirement income.

Now, I know this might seem like a lot to digest, but understanding the link between economic growth and COLA is like having a secret decoder ring for your retirement finances. It helps you make sense of the financial news, anticipate potential changes in your benefits, and plan accordingly.

In the next section, we'll examine the long-term outlook for Social Security and COLA, exploring the challenges and opportunities that lie ahead.

3.3 Long-Term Outlook for Social Security and COLA

Now, I know what you might be thinking: "Long-term? Isn't that a bit, well, long?" But trust me, when it comes to retirement planning, it's never too early to start thinking about the big picture.

Think of it like this: Imagine you're planning a cross-country road trip. You wouldn't just focus on the next gas station, would you? You'd map out your route, consider potential detours, and make sure you have enough resources to reach your final destination.

Similarly, regarding Social Security and COLA, it's crucial to look beyond the immediate future and consider the long-term trends that might shape your retirement income.

Now, let's address the elephant in the room: Social Security's long-term solvency. You might have heard whispers about the program facing financial challenges in the coming decades. It's true that with longer lifespans and a shrinking workforce, Social Security's trust fund is projected to be depleted by the early 2030s.

But before you start panicking, let me assure you: This doesn't mean Social Security is going bankrupt. Even if the trust fund is depleted, ongoing payroll taxes will still be able to cover about 77% of promised benefits.

So, while some adjustments might be needed to ensure the program's long-term sustainability, Social Security isn't going away anytime soon.

Now, how does this affect COLA? One potential scenario is that future COLA increases might be smaller than we've seen in the past. This could happen if policymakers decide to adjust the COLA formula to reflect the program's financial constraints.

Another possibility is that the way COLA is calculated might change. Currently, as you know, COLA is based on the CPI-W, which measures the average price changes for a basket of goods and services consumed by urban wage earners and clerical workers.

However, some experts argue that the CPI-W doesn't accurately reflect the spending patterns of seniors, who tend to spend more on healthcare and housing. They propose using a different measure, the CPI-E (Consumer Price Index for the Elderly), which precisely tracks the spending habits of older Americans.

Switching to the CPI-E could result in higher COLA increases, as healthcare costs rise faster than other goods and services. However, this change would also increase the cost of Social Security, which could lead to other adjustments to ensure the program's long-term viability.

Now, I know what you might be thinking: "This all sounds a bit uncertain. How can I plan for my retirement when the future of Social Security and COLA seems so unclear?" That's a valid concern, and it highlights the importance of having a diversified retirement plan.

Don't put all your eggs in the Social Security basket. Build a substantial nest egg through savings and investments, explore other sources of retirement income, and stay informed about potential changes to Social Security and COLA.

Imagine you're a gardener. You wouldn't just plant one type of flower in your garden, would you? You'd diversify your plants, choosing varieties that bloom at different times and can withstand various weather conditions.

Similarly, diversification is critical in uncritical treatment planning. By having multiple sources of income and a flexible plan, you can weather any storms that might come your way, including potential changes to Social Security and COLA.

Now, let's talk about some positive developments that could brighten the long-term outlook for Social Security and COLA. One promising trend is the increasing awareness of retirement security issues among policymakers and the public.

There's growing recognition that Social Security is a vital lifeline for millions of Americans, and protecting its future is a top priority. That could lead to bipartisan efforts to strengthen the program and ensure its long-term solvency, which would ultimately benefit COLA adjustments as well.

Another positive factor is the potential for technological advancements to improve Social Security's efficiency and effectiveness. Imagine a future where you can access all your Social Security information online, track your benefits, and even estimate your future COLA increases with a few clicks.

This increased transparency and accessibility could empower beneficiaries to make informed decisions about their retirement planning and stay engaged with the program.

Let's not forget about the power of advocacy. By staying informed about Social Security issues, contacting your elected officials, and supporting organizations that advocate for seniors, you can help shape the program's future and ensure that COLA continues to provide a vital safety net for retirees.

So, while the long-term outlook for Social Security and COLA might seem uncertain at times, there's also reason for optimism. By understanding the challenges, staying informed about potential changes, and taking a proactive approach to your retirement planning, you can navigate the future with confidence and enjoy the golden years you've worked so hard to achieve.

Part 2
Maximizing Your Social Security Benefits

Chapter 4
Understanding Your Full Retirement Age

Let's settle in for a chat about what might initially seem dry: Full Retirement Age (FRA). But don't worry—we'll keep it lively and jargon-free like we're planning a birthday party, not a tax audit!

Now, you might be thinking, "Retirement age? Isn't that 65? That's what my parents did." Well, it's not quite that simple anymore. Just like fashion trends and music styles, the concept of retirement age has evolved.

Think of it like this: Imagine you're baking a cake. You wouldn't just pull it out of the oven whenever you feel like it, would you? You'd follow the recipe, checking for doneness and making sure it's perfectly baked before you frost it.

Similarly, when it comes to Social Security, your FRA is like the recipe's baking time. It's the age at which you're entitled to receive your full, unreduced retirement benefits, the culmination of all those years you've paid into the system.

Now, here's the thing: your FRA isn't a one-size-fits-all number. It depends on when you were born. For most of us reading this book, it's likely somewhere between 66 and 67.

If you were born between 1943 and 1954, your FRA is 66. But if you were born in 1960 or later, it's 67. For those born between 1955 and 1959, it falls somewhere in between, gradually increasing from 66 and 2 months to 66 and 10 months.

You can find your exact FRA on your Social Security statement or by using the handy-dandy online calculator on the Social Security Administration's website (ssa.gov). It's like a personalized birthday card from Uncle Sam, telling you when it's time to claim your full benefits.

Now, you might be wondering, "Why is this FRA so important? Can't I just start collecting benefits whenever I feel like retiring?" Well, you can, but there's a catch.

If you claim benefits before your FRA, your monthly payments will be permanently reduced. Think of it like getting a slightly smaller slice of the retirement pie. The earlier you claim, the smaller your slice will be.

For example, if your FRA is 67 and you start collecting benefits at 62, your monthly payments will be reduced by about 30%. That's a significant chunk of change!

On the other hand, if you delay claiming benefits past your FRA, your monthly payments will increase. It's like getting a bonus slice of pie for being patient. For each year you delay claiming, your benefits will increase by about 8% until you reach age 70.

So, as you can see, understanding your FRA is crucial for making informed decisions about when to start collecting Social Security. It's like knowing the rules of the game before you start playing.

Now, I know what you might be thinking: "This is all starting to sound like a math problem!" And you're right; there are some calculations involved. But don't worry; we'll keep it simple and focus on the key concepts.

Think of your FRA as a balancing point. If you claim before your FRA, you will receive smaller monthly payments but more years of benefits collection. Delaying past your FRA will result in larger monthly payments but fewer years of benefits collection.

The best strategy for you will depend on your circumstances, including your health, financial needs, and life expectancy. It's like choosing the right pair of shoes for a hike. You need to consider the terrain, the weather, and your personal preferences to find the best fit.

In the next section, we'll explore the pros and cons of early vs. late claiming, helping you weigh the options and make the best decision for your retirement journey.

4.2 Early vs. Late Claiming: Weighing the Options

Let's dive into one of the most crucial decisions you'll face on your Social Security journey: when to start claiming those hard-earned benefits. It's like choosing the perfect time to harvest a ripened fruit – pick too early, and it might be sour; wait too long, and it mig

As we discussed earlier, your Full Retirement Age (FRA) is the sweet spot where you can receive your full, unreduced benefits. However, the Social Security system offers some flexibility, allowing you to claim benefits as early as 62 or delay them as late as 70.

Now, you might be thinking, "Why wouldn't I just start collecting as soon as possible? More money sooner, right?" Well, it's not quite that simple. Claiming comes with a trade-off: your monthly payments will be permanently reduced.

Think of it like this: Imagine you have a birthday cake, and you can choose to cut yourself a slice now or wait until later. If you're impatient and grab a slice right away, you'll get a smaller piece. But if you wait, you might get a bigger, more satisfying slice later.

Similarly, with Social Security, claiming means smaller monthly checks, while delaying means larger payments. It's a balancing act, and the best choice for you will depend on your circumstances.

Let's explore the pros and cons of each option:

Claiming Early (before your FRA):

Pros:

- **More years to enjoy your benefits:** You'll start receiving payments sooner, giving you more time to use the money for travel, hobbies, or whatever your heart desires.
- **A financial cushion if you need it:** If you're facing financial hardship or need to supplement your income, claiming can provide a much-needed boost.
- **Peace of mind:** For some, the security of knowing they have a guaranteed income stream, even if it's reduced, outweighs the potential for larger payments later.

Cons:

- **Smaller monthly payments:** Your benefits will be permanently reduced, which could significantly impact your retirement income, especially if you live a long life.
- **Potential impact on spousal benefits:** If you're married, claiming could also reduce your spouse's survivor benefits, which they might rely on if you pass away first.
- **Missed opportunity for larger payments:** If you delay claiming, your benefits will increase, potentially providing a more substantial income stream later in retirement.

Delaying Benefits (past your FRA):

Pros:

- **Larger monthly payments:** Your benefits will increase each year you delay, potentially providing a more comfortable retirement lifestyle.
- **Increased survivor benefits:** If you're married, delaying your benefits can also increase your spouse's survivor benefits, providing them with greater financial security if you pass away first.
- **Protection against inflation:** Larger monthly payments can help you better cope with rising costs in the future.

Cons:

- **Fewer years to collect benefits:** You'll receive payments for a shorter period, which could mean missing out on potential income if you live a long life.
- **Opportunity cost:** You might miss out on the chance to use the money earlier in retirement for travel, hobbies, or other expenses.
- **Uncertainty about the future:** You can't predict how long you'll live or what your financial needs will be in the future.

Now, I know what you're thinking: "How do I decide which option is right for me?" Well, it's like choosing the right tool for a job. You need to consider the specific task at hand and the tools available to you.

Similarly, when deciding when to claim Social Security, you need to assess your , including:

- **Your health and life expectancy:** If you expect to live a long life, delaying benefits might be an excellent strategy to maximize your lifetime income. But if you have health concerns, claiming might make more sense.
- **Your financial needs:** If you need the money now to cover expenses or supplement your income, claiming early might be necessary. But if you have other sources of income and can afford to wait, delaying might be a better option.
- **Your spouse's situation:** If you're married, consider your spouse's age, health, and potential survivor benefits when deciding.
- **Your personal preferences:** Some people value the peace of mind of having a guaranteed income stream sooner, while others prefer the potential for larger payments later. Your personal preferences should also play a role in your decision.

It's like planning a vacation. You need to consider your budget, your travel style, and your desired destinations to create the perfect itinerary. Similarly, when it comes to Social Security, there's no one-size-fits-all answer. The best strategy aligns with your individual needs and goals.

4.3 Spousal Benefits and Survivor Benefits

Let's have a heart-to-heart discussion about a topic that's overlooked in social Social securitization: spousal benefits and survivor benefits. Now, it might not sound as exciting as planning a dream vacation with your retirement funds, but trust me, these benefits are a crucial safety net, especially for married couples.

Think of Social Security as a family affair. It's not just about you; it's about protecting your loved ones and ensuring their financial well-being, even when you're no longer around. That's where spousal benefits and survivor benefits come into play.

Let's start with spousal benefits. Imagine you and your spouse have been a team for decades, navigating life's ups and downs together. You've both worked hard and paid into Social Security, and now it's time to enjoy the fruits of your labor.

But here's the thing: sometimes, one spouse might have a lower lifetime earning record than the other. They may have taken time off to raise children, care for an aging parent, or simply work in a lower-paying field.

That's where spousal benefits step in to provide a helping hand. If you're married or have been married for at least 10 years, you may be eligible to receive benefits based on your spouse's work record, even if you have little or no work history of your own.

Think of it like a shared retirement plan, a way to ensure both partners have a decent income in their golden years. The spousal benefit can be up to 50% of your spouse's total retirement benefit amount.

Here's where things get more nuanced. To receive spousal benefits, your spouse must already be receiving their retirement benefits. And the amount you receive will depend on your work history and when you choose to claim benefits.

If you claim spousal benefits before your own FRA, your payments will be reduced, just like with regular retirement benefits. But if you wait until your FRA, you'll receive the total spousal benefit amount.

Now, let's talk about survivor benefits. Life is unpredictable, and sadly, one spouse might pass away before the other. In these challenging times, Social Security provides a lifeline for the surviving spouse and any dependent children.

Survivor benefits are a way to ensure that your loved ones are taken care of financially, even when you're no longer there to provide for them. They can help cover living expenses, pay for education, and give a sense of security during a challenging time.

The amount of survivor benefits a spouse can receive depends on the deceased spouse's work record and when the surviving spouse chooses to claim benefits. If the surviving spouse waits until their FRA, they can receive 100% of the deceased spouse's benefit amount.

But here's an important point: claiming strategies for spousal and survivor benefits can be complex and depend on various factors, including your age, your spouse's age, your work history, and your individual financial needs.

It's like planning a family road trip. You need to consider everyone's preferences, pack enough snacks, and map out a route that works for everyone. Similarly, when it comes to spousal and survivor benefits, it's crucial to plan carefully and consider all the options.

Here are a few key things to keep in mind:

- **Coordinate your claiming strategies:** If you're married, talk to your spouse about your Social Security options and coordinate your claiming strategy to maximize your combined benefits.
- **Consider your life expectancy:** If you expect to live a long life, delaying benefits might be an excellent strategy to increase your spouse's survivor benefits.
- **Remember dependent children:** If you have children under 18, they may also be eligible for survivor benefits, which can help cover their expenses and education costs.

- **Seek professional guidance:** If you're unsure about the best claiming strategy for your family, consider consulting a financial advisor or Social Security specialist. They can help you navigate the complexities and make informed decisions.

Think of spousal and survivor benefits as a safety net woven with love and care. They're a way to protect your family's financial well-being, even in the face of life's uncertainties. By understanding these benefits and planning wisely, you can ensure that your loved ones are taken care of, no matter what the future holds.

Chapter 5
Earnings Limits and How They Affect Your Benefits

Now, let's talk about something that might seem a bit ng at first: working while receiving Social Security benefits. You might be thinking for a minute, but isn't Social Security for retirement? Why would I work if I'm retired?"

Well, the truth is retirement doesn't always mean a complete stop to working. Many people choose to continue working part-time, pursue a passion project, or simply stay active and engaged in their communities. And that's perfectly fine! Social Security allows you to work and receive benefits, but there are a few rules to keep in mind.

Imagine you're a seasoned gardener with a beautiful flower bed. You've nurtured your plants and watched them grow, and now it's time to enjoy their blooms. But you also know that a bit of pruning and weeding can help those flowers thrive even more.

Similarly, working while receiving Social Security can be like tending to your retirement garden. It can provide extra income, keep you mentally and physically active, and even boost your social connections.

But just as over-pruning can harm your plants, exceeding the earnings limits can affect your benefits.

So, what are these earnings limits? Well, they're like speed limits on the retirement highway. If you stay within the limits, you're good to go. But if you exceed them, you might get a "ticket" in the form of reduced benefits.

For 2025, if you're under your full retirement age (FRA), you can earn up to $21,240 without affecting your benefits. But for every $2 you earn above that limit, $1 will be deducted from your Social Security payments.

Now, don't worry; this deduction isn't a penalty. It's more like a temporary withholding. Once you reach your FRA, the withheld benefits will be recalculated to give you credit for those months when your payments were reduced. Think of it as a delayed gratification plan, where you're rewarded for working and contributing to the system.

But here's where things get a bit more nuanced. In the year you reach your FRA, the earnings limit increases. For 2025, if you reach your FRA during the year, you can earn up to $56,520 without affecting your benefits. For every $3 you earn above that limit, $1 will be deducted from your payments.

And once you reach your FRA, there's no earnings limit at all! You can work as much as you like and still receive your full Social Security benefits. It's like getting a green light to pursue your passions and earn extra income without worrying about affecting your retirement payments.

Now, I know what you might be thinking: "These rules seem complicated! How do I keep track of everything?" Well, the Social Security Administration (SSA) has your back. They provide online tools and resources to help you understand the earnings limits and track your earnings throughout the year.

You can also call the SSA or visit a local office for personalized guidance. Think of them as your retirement navigators, helping you stay on course and avoid unexpected detours.

And here's a friendly reminder: it's essential to report your earnings to the SSA, even if you think you're below the limits. That helps ensure that your benefits are calculated accurately and that you receive the correct payments.

Now, let's talk about some real-life examples to see how these earnings limits work in practice.

Imagine Sarah, a retired teacher who loves working with children. She decides to take a part-time job at a local daycare, earning $18,000 per year. Since she's under her FRA and her earnings are below the limit, her Social Security benefits won't be affected. She can enjoy the extra income and the satisfaction of continuing to make a difference in her community.

Now, let's meet David, a retired carpenter who enjoys staying active. He decides to start a small woodworking business, earning $30,000 per year. Since he's also under his FRA and his earnings exceed the limit, some of his benefits will be withheld. However, once he reaches his FRA, those withheld benefits will be recalculated, and his monthly payments will increase.

As you can see, working while receiving Social Security can be a great way to stay active, engaged, and financially secure in retirement. But it's essential to understand the rules of the road and plan accordingly. By staying informed and seeking guidance when needed, you can navigate the earnings limits with confidence and enjoy the best of both worlds – the rewards of work and the security of Social Security.

5.2 Strategies for Working While Receiving Social Security

We've talked about the rules of the road when it comes to working while receiving Social Security, those earnings limits that can sometimes feel like a puzzle. But fear not, fellow traveler, for there are strategies and detours to help you navigate this terrain and make the most of your retirement journey.

Imagine you're planning a road trip. You wouldn't just hop in the car and start driving without a map, would you? Consider different routes, scenic detours, and maybe even a few rest stops along the way to make the journey more enjoyable.

Similarly, it's wise to have a strategy in place for working while receiving Social Security. This roadmap helps you maximize your benefits and achieve your retirement goals.

One strategy is to **time your work and make decisions carefully**. If you're approaching your FRA and considering working part-time, you should delay claiming your benefits until you reach that magical age. This way, you can earn extra income without worrying about those pesky earnings limits affecting your payments.

It's like choosing the best time to plant your garden. You wouldn't sow seeds in the middle of winter, would you? You'd wait for the optimal conditions when the soil is warm, and the sun is shining. Similarly, timing your work and making decisions strategically can help you reap the maximum benefits from both.

Another strategy is to **explore different types of work**. Retirement doesn't have to mean a complete stop to earning income. It could be a chance to pursue a passion project, turn a hobby into a side hustle, or even volunteer your skills and experience to make a difference in your community.

Think of it like exploring a new city. You wouldn't just stick to the main tourist attractions, would you? You'd venture off the beaten path, discover hidden gems, and experience the city's unique charm. Similarly, retirement can be a time to explore new avenues, discover hidden talents, and find fulfilling ways to contribute your skills.

If you're passionate about teaching, you could offer tutoring services or teach online courses. If you love crafting, you could sell your creations at local markets or online platforms. If you enjoy helping others, you could volunteer at a local charity or mentor young people.

The possibilities are endless, and the beauty of it is that you can tailor your work to your interests, skills, and desired income level. It's like creating a custom-made suit for your retirement lifestyle.

Another strategy is to **be mindful of your earnings throughout the year**. Remember those earnings limits we talked about? Well, it's essential to keep track of your income and ensure you don't exceed those limits if you're under your FRA.

Think of it like managing your household budget. You wouldn't spend recklessly without keeping an eye on your bank account, would you? You'd track your expenses, make adjustments as needed, and ensure you're staying within your financial means.

Similarly, when working while receiving Social Security, it's crucial to monitor your earnings, especially if you're close to the limits. You can use the SSA's online tools or consult with a financial advisor to stay on track and avoid any surprises when it comes to your benefits.

And here's a pro tip: if you're approaching your FRA and expect to exceed the earnings limit, consider delaying your Social Security claiming until the following year. This way, you can maximize your earnings without affecting your benefits. It's like timing your harvest to ensure you get the most out of your crops.

Another strategy is to **communicate with the SSA**. If you have any questions or concerns about working while receiving benefits, don't hesitate to reach out to the SSA. They're there to help you navigate the rules and make informed decisions.

Think of them as your retirement coaches, providing guidance and support along the way. You can get the information you need by calling them, visiting a local office, or even using their online resources.

And remember, life is full of surprises. If your work situation changes unexpectedly, let the SSA know. They can help you adjust your benefits and ensure you're receiving the correct payments.

By being proactive, informed, and strategic, you can successfully navigate the world of working while receiving Social Security. It's about finding the right balance between earning income, pursuing your passions, and enjoying the benefits you've earned.

Think of it as a dance, a graceful interplay between work and retirement. With the proper steps and a bit of planning, you can create a harmonious rhythm that allows you to thrive in your golden years.

5.3 Taxation of Social Security Benefits

Let's tackle a topic that often makes people cringe: taxes. But don't worry, we're not going to get bogged down in complicated forms and confusing jargon. We'll keep it simple, like a friendly chat about how to keep more of your hard-earned Social Security benefits in your pocket.

You might be surprised to learn that those monthly checks you receive from Social Security might not be entirely tax-free. It depends on your overall income level and a few other factors. Think of it like this: imagine you're baking a cake, and you have a certain amount of flour to work with. Depending on the size of your cake and how many other ingredients you add, you might have some flour left over, or you might need to use it all.

Similarly, with Social Security, your benefits are like the flour, and your other income sources are like the other ingredients. Depending on the size of your "cake" (your combined income), you might have some of your benefits left over after taxes or need to pay taxes on a portion of them.

Now, how does the government decide how much of your benefits are taxable? Well, they use a formula based on your "combined income," which includes your adjusted gross income, nontaxable interest income, and half of your Social Security benefits.

If your combined income is below a certain threshold, your benefits are not taxed at all. That's like having enough flour left over to bake another cake! But if your combined income exceeds that threshold, a portion of your benefits may be subject to federal income tax.

For 2025, these are the thresholds:
- **Individual filers:** If your combined income is less than $32,000, your benefits are not taxed. If it's between $32,000 and $44,000, up to 50% of your benefits may be taxable. And if it's over $44,000, up to 85% of your benefits may be taxable.
- **Joint filers:** If your combined income is less than $44,000, your benefits are not taxed. If it's between $44,000 and $64,000, up to 50% of your benefits may be taxable. And if it's over $64,000, up to 85% of your benefits may be taxable.

Now, I know what you might be thinking: "This is getting complicated!" But don't worry, it's not as daunting as it seems. The IRS provides worksheets and instructions to help you calculate your taxable benefits, and you can also use tax software or consult with a tax professional for assistance.

Think of it like following a recipe. You might need to measure out the ingredients carefully and follow the instructions step-by-step, but with a bit of patience and guidance; you can bake a delicious cake (or, in this case, manage your taxes effectively).

And here's a friendly reminder: not everyone pays taxes on their Social Security benefits. In fact, a significant portion of beneficiaries don't owe any taxes on their payments. It all depends on your income situation.

Let's look at life examples to see how this works in practice.

Imagine Sarah, a retired teacher who receives $1,800 per month in Social Security benefits. She also has some savings that generate $5,000 in interest income per year. Her combined income is below the threshold for taxation, so she doesn't owe any taxes on her Social Security benefits.

Now, let's meet David, a retired engineer who receives $2,200 per month in Social Security benefits and has a part-time job that earns him $25,000 per year. His combined income exceeds the threshold, so a portion of his benefits may be subject to federal income tax.

As you can see, the taxation of Social Security benefits depends on your circumstances. It's essential to understand the rules, calculate your combined income, and plan accordingly.

And here's a pro tip: if you're concerned about the potential tax implications of your Social Security benefits, consider exploring strategies to reduce your taxable income. This might include contributing to tax-deferred retirement accounts, like a 401(k) or IRA, or taking advantage of other tax deductions and credits.

Think of it like finding creative ways to save money on your grocery bill. Use coupons, buy in bulk, or shop at discount stores to stretch your budget further. Similarly, with taxes, there are strategies you can use to minimize your tax liability and keep more of your hard-earned money.

By understanding the rules of the game and planning strategically, you can navigate the world of Social Security taxation with confidence and ensure that you're maximizing your benefits while fulfilling your tax obligations. It's all about being informed, proactive, and resourceful, just like a savvy shopper who knows how to get the best deals and make their money work harder for them.

Chapter 6
Integrating Social Security with Pensions and Retirement Savings

Think of your retirement income like a delicious stew. You wouldn't want it to be made of just one ingredient, would you? You can add a variety of spices and meat to create a flavorful and satisfying meal.

Similarly, when it comes to planning your retirement income, it's wise to have a mix of different sources, not just rely solely on Social Security. It's about creating a recipe for financial security, blending different ingredients to achieve a well-balanced and fulfilling retirement.

Social Security is like the potatoes in your stew – a hearty and reliable base. But to make it truly satisfying, you'll want to add other ingredients, like pensions and retirement savings, to enhance the flavor and provide a more robust and fulfilling experience.

Pensions are like the carrots in your stew – a nutritious and dependable addition. They're a type of retirement plan offered by some employers, where you and your employer contribute money during your working years, and you receive a guaranteed income stream in retirement.

Think of it as a deferred compensation plan, where you're saving a portion of your salary for your future self. Pensions provide a predictable income stream, which can be a valuable complement to your Social Security benefits.

Now, here's where things get interesting. The way you integrate your pension with Social Security can significantly impact your overall retirement income. If you have a pension, it's crucial to coordinate your claiming strategies to maximize your benefits.

For example, if your pension provides a substantial income stream, consider delaying your Social Security and claiming to increase your monthly payments later. That can help you create a more balanced income stream throughout your retirement.

On the other hand, if your pension is smaller or you have different financial needs, claiming Social Security earlier makes more sense to provide a steady income stream while you're still young and active.

It's like choosing the right spices for your stew. You wouldn't add a whole jar of chili powder if you prefer a milder flavor, would you? You carefully select the spices that complement the other ingredients and create the desired taste.

Similarly, when coordinating your pension with Social Security, you must consider your individual preferences, financial needs, and overall retirement goals.

Now, let's talk about another critical ingredient in your retirement stew: retirement savings. Think of these as the flavorful herbs and spices that add depth and complexity to your meal.

Retirement savings come in various forms, like 401(k)s, IRAs, and other investment accounts. They're like personal piggy banks where you save and invest money during your working years, allowing it to grow and provide a nest egg for your retirement.

Unlike pensions, which provide a guaranteed income stream, retirement savings offer more flexibility and control. You can choose how to invest your money, adjust your contributions as needed, and even withdraw funds early if necessary (although there might be penalties involved).

Integrating your retirement savings with Social Security can be like adding the perfect finishing touch to your stew. It's about creating a harmonious blend of income sources that provides both stability and flexibility in your retirement.

One strategy is to use your retirement savings to supplement your Social Security benefits, especially in the early years of retirement when you might be more active and have higher expenses. That can help you maintain your lifestyle and pursue your passions without depleting your savings too quickly.

Another strategy is to use your retirement savings to create a buffer against unexpected expenses or financial emergencies. Life is full of surprises, and having a financial cushion can provide peace of mind and help you weather any storms that might come your way.

Think of it like having a spare tire in your car. You hope you'll never need it, but it's reassuring to know it's there just in case. Similarly, your retirement savings can be your financial spare tire, providing a safety net when you need it most.

And here's a pro tip: consider working with a financial advisor to create a personalized retirement plan that integrates your Social Security benefits, pension (if you have one), and retirement savings. They can help you assess your financial situation, project your income needs, and develop a strategy that aligns with your goals.

It's like having a master chef guide you through the recipe for a delicious and satisfying retirement stew. They can help you choose the right ingredients, adjust the seasonings, and create a culinary masterpiece that nourishes your financial well-being in your golden years.

6.2 Maximizing Your Income Streams in Retirement

Imagine your retirement income as a flowing river, constantly replenished by various tributaries. You wouldn't want it to be a stagnant pool, would you? You'd like a vibrant, dynamic flow of income to support your dreams and aspirations throughout your golden years.

Social Security is like the main channel of that river, providing a steady and reliable flow of income. But to make it genuinely abundant, you'll want to explore other tributaries and income streams that can enrich your retirement experience and provide financial security.

Imagine you're a skilled artisan crafting beautiful pottery. You wouldn't limit yourself to just one type of clay or glaze, would you? You'd experiment with different materials, techniques, and designs to create a diverse and captivating collection.

Similarly, in retirement, you can explore various income-generating opportunities to diversify your financial portfolio and create a more vibrant and fulfilling life.

One option is to **continue working part-time**. Retirement doesn't have to mean a complete stop to your professional life. It could be a chance to pursue a passion project, share your expertise as a consultant, or simply enjoy the social interaction and mental stimulation of a part-time job.

Think of it like tending to a small garden patch. You might not be cultivating a whole farm, but you're still nurturing your skills, enjoying the fruits of your labor, and reaping the rewards of a fulfilling activity. Working part-time can provide a valuable income stream, supplement your Social Security benefits, and even boost your sense of purpose and well-being. It's a way to stay active, engaged, and connected to the world around you.

Another option is to **turn your hobbies into income-generating activities**. Do you love baking, knitting, or woodworking? You may have a knack for photography, writing, or gardening. Retirement can be a time to turn those passions into profit.

Think of it as opening a small shop in your neighborhood, sharing your creations with the world, and earning income from your talents. You can sell your crafts online, at local markets, or even through word-of-mouth referrals.

Not only can this provide a financial boost, but it can also bring immense satisfaction and joy. It's a way to turn your passions into a source of both income and fulfillment.

And here's a thought: have you considered **renting out a spare room or property**? If you have extra space in your home or own a vacation property, renting it out can be a lucrative way to generate income in retirement.

Think of it as welcoming guests into your home, sharing your space, and creating a welcoming environment for travelers or long-term renters. It can provide a steady income stream, help you cover your expenses, and even create new social connections.

With the rise of online platforms like Airbnb and Vrbo, renting out your property has never been easier. Through a user-friendly interface, you can manage bookings, communicate with guests, and even receive payments.

Another option is to **explore the world of investing**. Retirement can be a time to use your financial knowledge and grow your nest egg through intelligent investments.

Think of it like planting seeds in a fertile garden, nurturing them with care, and watching them blossom into a bountiful harvest. Investing can help you build wealth, protect your savings from inflation, and even create a legacy for future generations.

Investing involves risks, and it's essential to do your research, seek professional advice if needed, and choose investments that align with your risk tolerance and financial goals. But with careful planning and a long-term perspective, investing can be a powerful tool to maximize your income streams in retirement.

And here's a thought: have you considered **annuities**? They're like insurance policies for your retirement income, providing a guaranteed stream of payments for a specified period or even for the rest of your life.

Think of it as a pension you create for yourself, providing a predictable income stream that you can rely on no matter how long you live.

Annuities can be a valuable addition to your retirement portfolio, especially if you're concerned about outliving your savings.

By exploring these various income-generating opportunities, you can create a diversified and dynamic retirement income stream. It's about being creative, resourceful, and proactive, just like a skilled artisan who uses their talents to create a masterpiece.

Retirement is not just a time to relax and enjoy the fruits of your labor. It's also an opportunity to explore new avenues, pursue your passions, and continue to grow and thrive financially. By maximizing your income streams, you can create a retirement that is both fulfilling and financially secure.

6.3 Creating a Diversified Retirement Portfolio

Imagine you're a farmer preparing for the harvest season. You wouldn't just plant one type of crop, would you? You'd diversify your fields, sowing different seeds that thrive in various conditions. That way, if one crop fails due to drought or pests, you still have others to rely on.

Similarly, diversification is critical to building a retirement portfolio. It's about spreading your investments across different asset classes, like stocks, bonds, and real estate, to create a resilient and balanced financial ecosystem.

Think of your retirement portfolio as a garden, with each investment representing a different type of plant. Stocks are like vibrant flowers, offering the potential for high growth but also carrying some risk. Bonds are like sturdy shrubs, providing stability and income. Real estate is like strong trees, offering long-term value and potential for appreciation.

By diversifying your portfolio, you create a balanced ecosystem where different investments can thrive in various economic conditions. If the stock market takes a downturn, your bonds and real estate might provide stability. If interest rates rise, your stocks offer growth potential.

It's like having a well-rounded team of players on a sports field. Each player has their strengths and weaknesses, but together, they create a winning combination. Similarly, different asset classes work together in your retirement portfolio to provide a balanced and resilient approach to financial security.

Now, you might be wondering, "How do I know which investments are right for me?" Well, it's like choosing the right plants for your garden.

You need to consider your climate, soil conditions, and personal preferences to create a thriving landscape.

Similarly, when building your retirement portfolio, you need to consider your risk tolerance, time horizon, and financial goals. If you're younger and have a longer time horizon, you might be more comfortable with riskier investments, like stocks, that offer higher growth potential.

But suppose you're closer to retirement or prefer a more conservative approach. In that case, you might opt for a more significant allocation to bonds, which offer stability and income but typically have lower growth potential.

And don't forget about real estate. Investing in property is a great way to diversify your portfolio and generate rental income or appreciation over time. It's like owning a piece of the land, a tangible asset that can provide stability and security.

Now, here's where Social Security comes into play. Think of it as the fertile soil that nourishes your retirement garden. It provides a solid foundation for your income, allowing you to take a more balanced approach to your investments.

With Social Security as your safety net, you might feel more comfortable taking on some risk in your portfolio, knowing that you have a guaranteed income stream to fall back on. It's like having a safety harness while climbing a mountain. You can explore new heights with confidence, knowing that you have a backup plan in case of a misstep.

But remember, Social Security is just one piece of the puzzle. To create a truly diversified and resilient retirement portfolio, you must consider all the pieces and how they fit together.

It's like building a house. You wouldn't just focus on the foundation, would you? You'd also need strong walls, a sturdy roof, and a beautiful garden to create a complete and comfortable home.

Similarly, in retirement planning, you need a holistic approach that considers all aspects of your financial well-being. This includes not just Social Security and investments but also factors like healthcare costs, housing expenses, and potential long-term care needs.

By creating a diversified retirement portfolio, you're building a financial fortress. This strong and resilient structure can withstand economic uncertainty and provide a haven for your golden years.

It's about taking a proactive approach, understanding your options, and seeking guidance when needed. Think of it like embarking on a grand adventure, with Social Security as your compass and your diversified portfolio as your trusty map.

With careful planning and a bit of courage, you can confidently navigate the twists and turns of retirement, knowing that you have a well-balanced and resilient financial plan to guide you.

Part 3
Planning for a Secure Retirement

Chapter 7
Estimating Your Retirement Expenses

Imagine you're planning a road trip. You wouldn't just hit the gas and hope for the best, would you? You'd map out your route, estimate the distance, and calculate how much fuel you'll need to reach your destination.

Similarly, estimating your expenses is like charting your financial journey when it comes to retirement planning. It's about understanding how much money you'll need to maintain your lifestyle, pursue your passions, and enjoy your golden years without running out of fuel.

Now, you might be thinking, "Retirement expenses? That's easy! I'll just spend less than I do now." While that's a good starting point, it's not always that simple. Retirement can bring unexpected twists and turns, like healthcare costs, home repairs, or even the desire to travel and explore new hobbies.

Imagine you're moving into a new home. You might know how much space you need and what your furniture will look like in each room. But once you start unpacking and settling in, you might realize you need extra storage, a different layout, or even a new coat of paint.

Similarly, retirement can bring unexpected changes to your spending habits. That daily commute might be replaced with leisurely walks in the park, but those expensive lattes and lunches might turn into home-cooked meals and afternoon tea parties.

The key is anticipating these changes and creating a realistic budget that reflects your retirement lifestyle.

One way to estimate your retirement expenses is to use the "80% rule." This rule of thumb suggests that you'll need about 80% of your pre-retirement income to maintain your current standard of living.

If you're currently earning $60,000 per year, you need around $48,000 annually in retirement. This rule provides a good starting point, but it's important to remember that it's just an estimate. Your actual expenses might be higher or lower depending on your circumstances.

Think of it like a recipe. You might start with a basic recipe for a cake, but you might adjust the ingredients and measurements based on your preferences and dietary needs. Similarly, the 80% rule is a good starting point, but you might need to tweak it based on your unique situation.

Another approach is to track your current expenses and identify areas where you might spend more or less in retirement. This can help you create a more personalized and accurate budget.

For example, if you're planning to downsize your home or relocate to a more affordable area, your housing costs might decrease. On the other hand, if you're planning to travel extensively or pursue expensive hobbies, your leisure expenses might increase.

It's like planning a garden. You'd consider the size of your yard, the types of plants you want to grow, and the amount of sunlight and water they need. Similarly, when estimating your retirement expenses, you must consider your lifestyle, hobbies, and individual needs.

And don't forget about healthcare costs. Healthcare expenses tend to increase as we age, and it's crucial to factor them into your retirement budget. Medicare can help cover some of these costs, but you might also need to consider supplemental insurance or out-of-pocket expenses.

Think of it like preparing for a rainy day. You wouldn't leave the house without an umbrella, would you? Similarly, it's wise to have a financial umbrella to protect you from unexpected healthcare costs in retirement.

Now, you might wonder, "How does COLA fit into all of this?" Remember that COLA is designed to help your Social Security benefits keep pace with inflation. But it's not a magic bullet that will cover all your expenses.

It's like having a raincoat that protects you from the rain, but you might still need an umbrella for those heavy downpours. Similarly, COLA can help you maintain your purchasing power, but you still need a solid budget and other income sources to cover all your expenses.

By estimating your retirement expenses, you create a financial roadmap for your golden years. It's about understanding your needs, anticipating potential changes, and planning accordingly. It's a crucial step towards achieving a secure and fulfilling retirement, where you can enjoy your passions, pursue your dreams, and live life to the fullest without worrying about running out of fuel.

7.2 Building a Realistic Retirement Budget

Imagine you're building a house. You wouldn't just start stacking bricks without a blueprint, would you? You'd carefully plan the layout, estimate the materials needed, and create a budget to ensure you can afford your dream home.

Similarly, when it comes to retirement planning, a realistic budget is your blueprint for financial security. It's a roadmap that guides your spending, helps you prioritize your needs and wants, and ensures you can maintain your desired lifestyle throughout your golden years.

Think of your retirement budget as a balancing scale, with your income on one side and your expenses on the other. The goal is to keep those scales in equilibrium, ensuring your income comfortably covers your costs, with a little extra room for surprises.

Building a realistic retirement budget isn't about deprivation or penny-pinching. It's about making informed choices, prioritizing your spending, and finding creative ways to stretch your retirement income further.

It's like planning a road trip. You wouldn't just hit the gas and drive aimlessly, would you? You'd map out your route, estimate fuel costs, and plan for meals and accommodations along the way. Similarly, in retirement planning, a budget helps you navigate your journey, anticipate expenses, and ensure you have enough resources to reach your destination.

One of the first steps in building a realistic retirement budget is **assessing your current spending habits**. Look closely at your bank statements, credit card bills, and other financial records to get a clear picture of where your money is going.

Think of it like taking inventory of your pantry. You'd check your shelves, see what you have, and identify any expired or no longer needed items. Similarly, when reviewing your spending, you might discover areas where you can cut back, eliminate unnecessary expenses, or find more cost-effective alternatives.

Next, **consider how your expenses might change in retirement**. Some expenses, like commuting or work-related expenses, might decrease or disappear altogether. However, other costs, like healthcare or travel expenses, might increase as you have more time to pursue your passions and enjoy your freedom.

It's like planning a garden. You'd consider the different seasons, the types of plants you want to grow, and the resources they'll need to thrive. Similarly, in retirement planning, you must anticipate how your needs and expenses might evolve.

Now, here's where Social Security and COLA come into play. Your Social Security benefits will likely be a significant part of your retirement income, and the COLA adjustments will help those benefits keep pace with inflation.

But it's important to remember that COLA might not always cover all your expenses, especially if inflation is high or your spending habits change significantly. That's why it's crucial to **factor COLA into your budget projections** and be prepared for potential fluctuations and unexpected expenses.

Think of it like planning a picnic. You should check the weather forecast and pack a raincoat. Similarly, in retirement planning, it's wise to anticipate potential changes in your income and expenses so you can adjust your budget accordingly.

Another critical aspect of building a realistic retirement budget is **prioritizing your spending**. Not all expenses are created equal. Some are essential, like housing, food, and healthcare, and others are discretionary, like entertainment, travel, and hobbies.

It's like creating a grocery list. You'd prioritize essential items, like milk and bread, over non-essential treats, like ice cream and cookies. Similarly, in retirement planning, it's crucial to identify your essential expenses and ensure you can comfortably cover them before allocating funds to discretionary spending.

And here's a pro tip: **don't forget about those unexpected expenses** that can pop up like uninvited guests. Life is full of surprises, and retirement is no exception. You might face unexpected home repairs, medical bills, or even the need to help out a family member.

It's like having a rainy-day fund, a cash stash for those unexpected showers. Similarly, in retirement planning, it's wise to build a buffer into your budget to handle those unforeseen expenses without derailing your financial plans.

By creating a realistic retirement budget, you're building a solid financial foundation for your golden years. It's a roadmap that guides your spending, helps you prioritize your needs and wants, and ensures you can maintain your desired lifestyle throughout your retirement journey.

It's about being proactive, informed, and adaptable, just like a seasoned traveler who knows how to pack light, navigate detours, and enjoy the journey, even when unexpected challenges arise.

7.3 Adjusting Your Budget for Inflation and COLA Changes

Imagine you're a seasoned sailor navigating the open seas. You wouldn't just set sail without charting your course and anticipating potential changes in the weather, would you? You'd adjust your sails, navigate around storms, and stay vigilant to ensure a safe and successful voyage.

Similarly, when it comes to retirement planning, it's crucial to be adaptable and adjust your budget to navigate the ever-changing economic landscape. Inflation and COLA adjustments are like the winds and currents that can affect your financial journey, and it's essential to be prepared to adjust your sails accordingly.

Think of your retirement budget as a roadmap, guiding you toward your financial destination. But just like a roadmap needs to be updated to reflect new roads and detours, your budget needs to be flexible and adaptable to account for inflation and COLA changes.

As we've discussed, inflation is like a sneaky thief that can erode the purchasing power of your hard-earned money. It's like a hidden tax that silently increases the cost of everything from groceries and gas to healthcare and housing.

COLA, on the other hand, is like a friendly tailwind that helps you stay on course. It's designed to offset the impact of inflation on your Social Security benefits, ensuring that your income keeps pace with rising prices.

But here's the thing: COLA isn't always a perfect match for inflation. Sometimes, it might fall short, leaving a gap between your income and expenses. And that's where adjusting your budget becomes crucial.

Think of it as adjusting your sails to catch the wind more effectively. To navigate challenging economic conditions, you should trim your sails, change your course, or even drop anchor for a while.

Similarly, your retirement budget should be adjusted to account for inflation and COLA changes. This might involve reducing expenses, finding new sources of income, or even reconsidering your retirement timeline.

One strategy is to **track your spending and identify areas where you can cut back**. It's like taking inventory of your ship's supplies and identifying any unnecessary cargo that can be jettisoned to improve efficiency.

Look at your monthly expenses and see where you can trim the fat. Can you reduce your entertainment costs by dining out less often or finding more affordable alternatives for your hobbies? Can you negotiate lower rates for your insurance or find cheaper options for your utilities?

Every little bit helps, and even minor adjustments can add significant savings over time. It's like patching up small leaks in your ship to prevent it from using too much water.

Another strategy is to **explore ways to increase your income**. Retirement doesn't have to mean a complete stop to earning money. Consider part-time work, consulting, or even turning a hobby into a side hustle.

Think of it like setting up a fishing net to catch extra provisions during your voyage. It's about finding creative ways to supplement your income and keep your budget afloat.

If you enjoy working with people, consider a customer service role or a part-time position in retail. You could offer freelance services if you have a knack for writing or editing. If you're passionate about a particular subject, you could teach online courses or provide tutoring services.

The possibilities are endless, and the beauty is that you can tailor your work to your interests, skills, and desired income level. It's like discovering new fishing grounds that provide a bountiful catch.

Another strategy is to **re-evaluate your retirement timeline**. If you find it challenging to make ends meet, consider delaying your retirement or returning to work part-time.

Think of it like adjusting your course to avoid a storm. Sometimes, it's better to detour or wait for calmer waters before continuing your journey.

Delaying your retirement can give you more time to save and increase your Social Security benefits, while returning to work part-time can provide extra income and keep you mentally and physically active.

And here's a pro tip: **don't forget about the power of COLA**. While it might not always perfectly match inflation, it's a valuable tool that can help you maintain your purchasing power in retirement.

Keep an eye on COLA projections and factor them into your budget planning. If you anticipate a more minor COLA increase, be prepared to adjust your expenses or income to compensate.

Think of it like adjusting your sails to catch the wind more effectively. By anticipating changes in the economic climate, you can navigate your retirement journey with greater confidence and stability.

And remember, adjusting your budget is not a sign of failure. It's a sign of wisdom and adaptability, a willingness to navigate the challenges and embrace retirement's opportunities. It's about being proactive, resourceful, and resilient, just like a seasoned sailor who knows how to weather storms and reach their destination safely.

Chapter 8
Investment Options for Retirees

Imagine you're a chef preparing a grand feast. You wouldn't just use one ingredient, would you? You'd select a variety of fresh produce, flavorful spices, and perhaps some exotic ingredients to create a culinary masterpiece.

Similarly, when it comes to investing for retirement, it's wise to explore a diverse menu of investment options, each with its unique flavor and potential to enhance your financial well-being.

Think of your retirement portfolio as a recipe book filled with different investment options that can be combined to create a balanced and satisfying meal. Just as a chef carefully selects ingredients to complement each other, you'll want to choose investments that align with your risk tolerance, time horizon, and financial goals.

One of the most common investment options for retirees is **stocks**. Think of them as the spicy peppers in your recipe book – they can add a kick to your portfolio with their potential for high growth, but they also come with some heat in the form of volatility.

Stocks represent ownership in a company, and their value can fluctuate significantly depending on its performance, market conditions, and economic trends. In the investment world, stocks are like racehorses—they can be exciting and potentially lucrative but also unpredictable.

If you're comfortable with some risk and have a longer time horizon, stocks can be a valuable addition to your retirement portfolio. They can outpace inflation and grow your nest egg over time.

But it's important to remember that stocks can also lose value, especially in the short term. That's why it's crucial to diversify your stock holdings, investing in different companies, sectors, and even countries to spread your risk.

Think of it like adding a variety of peppers to your recipe – some might be mild, while others are fiery, but together, they create a balanced and flavorful dish.

Bonds are another staple in the retirement recipe book. Think of them as the calming herbs in your culinary creations—they provide stability and balance to your portfolio, offsetting the spiciness of stocks.

Bonds are like loans to governments or corporations. When you invest in a bond, you're lending money to the issuer in exchange for regular interest payments and the return of your principal at maturity.

Bonds are less risky than stocks, as their value fluctuates less. They're like the reliable workhorses in your investment stable – they might not be as flashy as racehorses, but they consistently get the job done.

If you're closer to retirement or prefer a more conservative approach, bonds can be a valuable addition to your portfolio. They offer a steady income stream and can help protect your nest egg from market volatility.

But it's important to remember that bonds also come with some risks, such as interest rates and inflation. Bond prices fall when interest rates rise, and when inflation is high, the fixed income from bonds might not keep pace with rising costs.

That's why it's crucial to diversify your bond holdings, investing in different types of bonds with varying maturities and credit ratings. It's like adding a variety of herbs to your recipe – each one brings its unique flavor and aroma to the dish.

Now, let's not forget about **real estate**. Think of it as the hearty root vegetables in your retirement feast – they provide a solid foundation and potential for long-term growth.

Investing in real estate can be a great way to diversify your portfolio and generate rental income or appreciation over time. It's like owning a piece of the land, a tangible asset that can provide stability and security.

However, real estate also comes with challenges, such as property management, maintenance costs, and market fluctuations. It's essential to carefully consider your investment goals and risk tolerance before venturing into the real estate market.

Think of it like cultivating a garden. You must prepare the soil, plant the seeds, and nurture your plants to ensure a bountiful harvest. Similarly, with real estate, you must research, choose suitable properties, and manage them effectively to reap the rewards.

And here's a bonus ingredient for your retirement recipe book: **alternative investments**. Think of these as exotic spices that add a touch of adventure and potential for higher returns to your portfolio.

Alternative investments include private equity, hedge funds, commodities, and even collectibles like art or vintage cars. In your investment world, they might be like adventurous explorers—they might venture off the beaten path, seeking unique opportunities and potentially higher rewards.

However, alternative investments also come with higher risks and often require specialized knowledge and expertise. It's essential to research, understand the risks involved, and seek professional advice before venturing into these uncharted territories.

Think of it like adding a pinch of exotic spice to your recipe – a little can go a long way, but too much can overpower the other flavors.

By carefully selecting and combining these various investment options, you can create a diversified and resilient retirement portfolio that aligns with your needs and goals. It's like crafting a culinary masterpiece, a symphony of flavors that nourishes your financial well-being and allows you to savor the fruits of your labor in retirement.

8.2 Balancing Risk and Return in Your Portfolio

Think of your retirement portfolio like a well-balanced meal. You wouldn't want to eat only spicy foods, would you? Mix in some milder dishes to create a satisfying and enjoyable dining experience.

Similarly, when it comes to investing for retirement, it's crucial to find the right balance between risk and return. You don't want to take on so much risk that you lose sleep at night, but you also don't want to be so conservative that your investments barely keep pace with inflation.

It's like walking a tightrope. You need to find the perfect balance between taking calculated risks to achieve your goals and staying secure enough to avoid a financial tumble.

Now, what exactly is risk in the investment world? It's the possibility that your investments could lose value. Some investments, like stocks, are riskier because their prices fluctuate significantly. However, they also offer the potential for higher returns over the long term.

Think of stocks like a roller coaster. They can take you on a thrilling ride with ups and downs that might make your heart race. But if you're in it for the long haul, you might enjoy the excitement and the potential for a rewarding experience.

Bonds, on the other hand, are like a leisurely train ride. They offer a smoother, more predictable journey with a lower potential for dramatic gains or losses. They're generally considered less risky than stocks but tend to have lower returns over time.

And then there's real estate, which is like owning a piece of land. It can provide stability and potential for appreciation, but it also comes with risks, such as property taxes, maintenance costs, and market fluctuations.

How do you find the right balance between these different investment options? It depends on your circumstances, including your risk tolerance, time horizon, and financial goals.

If you're younger and have a longer time horizon until retirement, you might be more comfortable taking on some risk. You have more time to recover from potential losses, and your investments have more time to grow.

Think of it like planting a tree. A young sapling might sway in the wind and face challenges as it grows, but it has plenty of time to develop strong roots and reach its full potential.

But if you're closer to retirement or prefer a more conservative approach, you might want to tilt your portfolio towards less risky investments, like bonds. This can help protect your nest egg and provide a steady income stream in your golden years.

It's like choosing a sturdy walking stick for a hike. It might not be the fastest way to travel, but it provides stability and support, helping you navigate the terrain confidently.

And don't forget about diversification. We've talked about this before, but it's worth repeating. Don't put all your eggs in one basket. Spread your investments across different asset classes to reduce overall risk and create a more resilient portfolio.

Think of it like building a house with a variety of materials. You wouldn't just use wood, would you? You'd also use concrete, steel, and other materials to create a strong and durable structure.

Similarly, different asset classes work together in your retirement portfolio to provide stability, growth potential, and protection against market fluctuations.

Now, here's where things get interesting. As you approach retirement, you should adjust your portfolio to reflect your changing needs and goals. You might shift towards a more conservative approach, reducing your exposure to riskier investments and focusing on generating income.

Think of it like preparing for a long journey. You might start with a fast car to cover more ground quickly, but as you get closer to your destination, you might switch to a more comfortable vehicle that prioritizes a smooth and steady ride.

Similarly, in retirement, you shift your investment strategy to prioritize stability and income generation, ensuring that your nest egg can support your lifestyle and provide peace of mind.

And don't forget about the role of Social Security in your overall retirement plan. It's like a reliable base camp, providing a guaranteed income stream that you can count on, no matter what the market throws your way.

With Social Security as your foundation, you can take a more balanced approach to your investments, knowing you have a safety net to fall back on. It's like having a warm and cozy cabin to return to after a long day of exploring the mountains.

By understanding the interplay between risk and return, diversifying your investments, and adjusting your strategy as needed, you can create a retirement portfolio that supports your goals, provides peace of mind, and allows you to enjoy your golden years to the fullest.

8.3 Protecting Your Investments from Inflation

Think of inflation as a sneaky termite, quietly gnawing away at the wooden foundation of your retirement dreams. You might not notice it at first, but it can weaken the structure and threaten your financial stability over time.

Like you'd protect your home from termites with preventative measures and regular inspections, you need to safeguard your investments from inflation's erosive effects. It's about building a resilient financial fortress that can withstand the test of time and economic fluctuations.

You might be thinking, "But how do I protect my investments from something as intangible as inflation?" Well, it's like choosing the suitable building materials for your house. You wouldn't build a house out of straw, would you? You'd use solid and durable materials that can withstand the elements.

Similarly, when it comes to investing, you want to choose assets that have the potential to outpace inflation, preserving your purchasing power and ensuring your nest egg doesn't shrink over time.

One strategy is to **diversify your investments across different asset classes**. Remember that garden analogy we talked about earlier? Well, it applies here as well. Don't put all your eggs in one basket. Spread your investments across stocks, bonds, real estate, and other asset classes to create a balanced and resilient portfolio.

As we discussed, stocks are like vibrant flowers in your garden. They offer the potential for high growth but also carry some risk. Over the long term, stocks have historically outpaced inflation, providing a hedge against rising prices.

But it's important to remember that stock markets can be volatile, with ups and downs that might make your heart skip a beat. That's why it's crucial to have a long-term perspective and not panic during market downturns.

Think of it like weathering a storm at sea. You might encounter rough waves and strong winds, but if you stay the course and keep your eyes on the horizon, you'll eventually reach calmer waters.

On the other hand, bonds are like the sturdy shrubs in your garden, providing stability and income. They're less volatile than stocks and offer a fixed income stream, which can be a valuable source of income in retirement.

But here's the thing: bonds can be vulnerable to inflation. If inflation rises, the fixed income from your bonds might not keep pace with rising prices, eroding your purchasing power over time.

That's why it's essential to consider **inflation-protected securities**, like Treasury Inflation-Protected Securities (TIPS). These bonds adjust their principal based on inflation, providing a guaranteed return that keeps pace with rising prices.

Think of them like adjustable-rate mortgages for your investments. As inflation rises, the principal of your TIPS increases, protecting your investment from the erosive effects of rising prices.

Another strategy is to **consider real estate**. Property investment can be a great way to hedge against inflation, as property values tend to rise over time. Plus, real estate can generate rental income, providing a steady stream of cash flow in retirement.

Think of it like owning a piece of the land, a tangible asset that can provide stability and security in an uncertain world. But remember, real estate also comes with its risks and responsibilities, so it's essential to research and invest wisely.

And don't forget about **alternative investments**, like commodities, precious metals, and even collectibles. These can provide diversification and potentially hedge against inflation, but they also carry their unique risks and complexities.

Think of them like adding exotic spices to your retirement stew. They can enhance the flavor and provide a unique twist, but it's essential to use them sparingly and understand their potential impact on your recipe.

Here's a crucial point: protecting your investments from inflation isn't just about choosing the right assets. It's also about **staying informed and adapting your strategy as needed**.

Think of it like being a vigilant gardener, constantly monitoring your plants, adjusting the watering schedule, and adding fertilizer when needed. Similarly, with your investments, you must stay informed about economic trends, monitor your portfolio's performance, and make adjustments to ensure it's aligned with your goals and risk tolerance.

This might involve rebalancing your portfolio periodically, shifting your asset allocation, or even seeking professional guidance from a financial advisor. It's about being proactive, adaptable, and informed, just like a seasoned gardener who can nurture their plants and create a thriving landscape.

By proactively protecting your investments from inflation, you're building a financial fortress that can withstand the test of time and economic fluctuations. It's about creating a resilient and balanced portfolio that provides security and peace of mind in retirement.

Chapter 9
Understanding Medicare and Supplemental Coverage

Consider retirement a grand adventure, a journey filled with new experiences, exciting opportunities, and perhaps a few unexpected twists and turns. But just like any adventure, it's wise to be prepared for the unexpected, especially regarding healthcare costs.

As we navigate the twists and turns of life, our healthcare needs tend to change. We may encounter unexpected illnesses, require specialized treatments, or need more support as we age. Those healthcare costs can add up quickly and strain our retirement budget.

That's where Medicare comes in, like a trusty first aid kit on your retirement adventure. It's a federal health insurance program that provides coverage for millions of Americans aged 65 and older and younger individuals with specific disabilities.

Think of Medicare as a safety net, a basic level of healthcare protection that helps you manage those unexpected medical expenses and ensures you have access to quality care when you need it most.

However, just like a first aid kit might not have everything you need for every situation, Medicare doesn't cover all healthcare costs. Supplemental coverage, like adding extra bandages and ointments to your kit, provides additional protection and peace of mind.

Medicare is divided into different parts, each covering specific types of healthcare services:

- **Part A (Hospital Insurance):** This covers inpatient hospital stays, skilled nursing facility care, hospice care, and home healthcare services. Think of it as your protection for those significant medical events requiring hospitalization or specialized care.
- **Part B (Medical Insurance):** This covers doctor visits, outpatient care, preventive services, and some medical equipment. Think of it as your routine checkups, those regular visits to your doctor to ensure you're staying healthy and catching any potential issues early on.
- **Part C (Medicare Advantage):** This is an alternative to Original Medicare (Parts A and B), offered by private insurance companies approved by Medicare. It typically includes Part A and Part B coverage and additional benefits like prescription

drug coverage and dental or vision care. Think of it as a bundled package, a one-stop shop for your healthcare needs.

- **Part D (Prescription Drug Coverage):** This helps cover the cost of prescription drugs. Think of it as your pharmacy benefit, ensuring you can afford the medications needed to stay healthy and manage chronic conditions.

Now, here's where supplemental coverage comes in. While Medicare provides a valuable foundation for your healthcare protection, it doesn't cover everything. There are deductibles, copayments, and coinsurance that you'll be responsible for, and some services might not be covered at all.

That's where Medigap policies, also known as Medicare Supplement Insurance, can help fill the gaps. These private insurance plans help pay for some out-of-pocket costs that Original Medicare doesn't cover.

Think of them as extra layers of protection, like adding a raincoat and umbrella to your adventure gear in case of unexpected showers. They can help you manage those healthcare costs and provide greater financial security in retirement.

Various Medigap plans are available, each offering different levels of coverage and benefits. It's essential to compare plans carefully and choose one that aligns with your healthcare needs and budget.

Another option for supplemental coverage is employer-sponsored retiree health insurance. If you're fortunate enough to have this benefit, it can provide valuable coverage and help reduce your out-of-pocket costs.

And don't forget about Medicaid, a joint federal and state program that helps with healthcare costs for people with limited income and resources. If you qualify for Medicaid, it can provide additional coverage and financial assistance.

Understanding Medicare and supplemental coverage can be like navigating a complex maze with different paths and options. But with a bit of guidance and research, you can find the right path for your healthcare needs and ensure you have the protection you need to enjoy your retirement adventure.

Think of it like planning your route for a hiking expedition. You'd research the terrain, pack the right gear, and hire a guide to help you navigate the trails. Similarly, with Medicare and supplemental coverage, it's essential to gather information, compare options, and seek guidance from trusted sources to make informed decisions.

Visit the official Medicare website (medicare.gov) for detailed information about the program, compare Medigap policies, and find answers to frequently asked questions. For personalized assistance, call Medicare directly or visit a local Social Security office.

And don't hesitate to reach out to your healthcare providers, insurance agents, or financial advisors for guidance. They can help you understand your options, navigate the enrollment process, and choose the coverage that best fits your needs and budget.

By understanding Medicare and supplemental coverage, you're equipping yourself with the knowledge and tools you need to navigate the healthcare landscape in retirement. It's about being proactive, informed, and prepared so you can enjoy your golden years with confidence and peace of mind, knowing you have the protection you need to face any unexpected healthcare challenges.

9.2 Estimating Healthcare Expenses in Retirement

Think of retirement planning as preparing for a long and exciting road trip. You'd map out your route, pack your bags, and ensure your car is tip-top. But you'd also be prepared for unexpected detours, flat tires, and maybe even a sudden change in the weather.

Similarly, when it comes to planning for retirement, it's crucial to anticipate those unexpected bumps in the road, especially regarding healthcare costs. These costs can be like a sudden hailstorm, catching you off guard and potentially derailing your financial plans if you're unprepared.

Estimating healthcare expenses in retirement can feel like gazing into a cloudy crystal ball. It's difficult to predict what your needs will be and how much they will cost. But just like a seasoned meteorologist can forecast weather patterns with reasonable accuracy, we can use available data and tools to estimate your potential healthcare expenses and prepare for those rainy days.

One way to approach this is to **consider the national averages**. According to Fidelity's latest Retiree Health Care Cost Estimate, a 65-year-old couple retiring in 2023 can expect to spend an average of $315,000 on healthcare throughout their retirement. That's a hefty sum to make anyone reach for their antacids!

But remember, this is just an average. Your actual expenses might be higher or lower depending on various factors, such as your health status, lifestyle choices, and where you live. Think of it like estimating your gas mileage for that road trip. The average mileage for your car model might be 30 miles per gallon, but your actual mileage will vary depending on your driving habits, the terrain, and whether you're cruising on the highway or stuck in city traffic.

Similarly, with healthcare costs, there are many variables at play. If you have a chronic condition like diabetes or heart disease, your expenses are likely to be higher than those of someone in excellent health. However, if you live a healthy lifestyle, exercise regularly, and eat a balanced diet, you can keep those costs lower.

And don't forget about where you live. Healthcare costs can vary significantly from state to state and even within different regions of the same state. If you live in a high-cost area, you might need to budget more for healthcare than someone in a more affordable region.

Now, you might wonder, "How can I get a more personalized estimate of my healthcare expenses?" Well, several online tools and resources can help you with this.

The **AARP's Health Care Costs Calculator** is a great place to start. It considers your age, health status, and location to provide a personalized estimate of your potential healthcare costs in retirement. Think of it like a GPS for your healthcare journey, providing directions and estimated costs for your specific route.

Another helpful tool is the **Medicare Plan Finder** on the Medicare website. This tool allows you to compare different Medicare plans and estimate out-of-pocket costs for various healthcare services. It's like having a personal shopper for Medicare, helping you find the best plan for your needs and budget.

Remember your own health history and family medical records. These can provide valuable clues about your potential healthcare needs in retirement. If your family has a history of heart disease or cancer, you might want to budget more for preventive screenings and possible treatments.

Think of it like studying your family's travel history. If your ancestors were prone to getting lost or taking detours, you should be extra careful with your navigation. Similarly, with healthcare, understanding your family's health history can help you anticipate potential challenges and plan accordingly.

Here's a crucial point: estimating healthcare expenses is not just about crunching numbers. It's also about understanding the healthcare costs you might encounter in retirement.

Think of it like packing your bags for that road trip. You wouldn't just throw in random items, would you? You'd carefully select the essentials, like clothes, toiletries, and maybe a first-aid kit, to be prepared for various situations.

Similarly, with healthcare, there are different types of costs to consider:
- **Premiums:** These are the monthly payments you make for your health insurance coverage, whether Medicare or a private plan.
- **Deductibles:** This is the amount you pay out-of-pocket before your insurance coverage kicks in.
- **Copayments and coinsurance** are the fixed amounts or percentages you pay for specific healthcare services, such as doctor visits or prescription drugs.
- **Out-of-pocket maximum:** This is the maximum amount you'll pay for covered healthcare expenses in a given year.

Understanding these different cost categories can help you create a more accurate budget and avoid financial surprises. Knowing the various types of terrain you might encounter on your road trip can also help you pack the right gear and be prepared for any challenges.

Remember, healthcare costs are not static. They tend to rise over time, often outpacing inflation. That's why it's crucial to factor in potential increases when estimating retirement expenses.

Think of it like anticipating rising gas prices during your road trip. You wouldn't want to run out of fuel in the middle of nowhere, would you? You'd factor in potential price increases and budget accordingly.

Similarly, with healthcare, it's wise to anticipate potential cost increases and build a buffer into your budget to account for those rising expenses. This might involve setting aside extra savings, exploring long-term care insurance options, or even considering lifestyle changes that can improve your health and reduce your healthcare needs.

Understanding the different types of healthcare costs, using available tools and resources, and factoring in potential increases can help you create a more accurate and resilient retirement budget. It's about being prepared, informed, and adaptable, just like a seasoned traveler who knows how to navigate the road ahead and reach their destination safely.

9.3 Strategies for Managing Healthcare Costs

Navigating the healthcare landscape in retirement can sometimes feel like venturing into a dense jungle, with unexpected costs lurking around every corner. But fear not, intrepid explorer, for there are strategies and tools to help you manage those costs and emerge from the wilderness with your financial health intact.

It's no secret that healthcare expenses can majorly drain your retirement budget. As we age, we tend to require more medical care, and those costs can add up quickly, especially if you encounter unexpected health challenges.

But just like a seasoned explorer would pack the right gear and prepare for potential challenges, you can take proactive steps to manage healthcare costs in retirement and protect your financial well-being.

One strategy is to **become an informed healthcare consumer**. It's like studying a map of the jungle, understanding the terrain, and identifying potential hazards before you embark on your journey.

Research different healthcare providers, compare costs, and understand your insurance coverage options. Don't hesitate to ask questions, negotiate prices, and seek second opinions when necessary.

You can also explore alternative healthcare options, like telemedicine or community health clinics, which offer more affordable services. It's like finding hidden trails and shortcuts that can help you navigate the jungle more efficiently.

Another strategy is to **prioritize preventive care**. It's like building a sturdy shelter to protect yourself from the elements. By taking care of your health and addressing potential issues early on, you can reduce the risk of costly medical emergencies down the road.

Get regular checkups, screenings, and vaccinations. Maintain a healthy lifestyle through exercise, a balanced diet, and stress management techniques. Don't hesitate to seek professional help if you have any health concerns.

Preventive care is like investing in your health and building a solid foundation to withstand aging challenges.

Another strategy is to **explore Medicare and supplemental insurance options**. Medicare is like a trusty compass that can guide you through the healthcare jungle in retirement. It's a federal health insurance program that provides coverage for seniors and individuals with disabilities.

But Medicare doesn't cover everything. That's where supplemental insurance, like Medigap or Medicare Advantage plans, comes into play. These plans can help fill the gaps in Medicare coverage, providing additional protection against unexpected costs.

Choosing the right Medicare and supplemental insurance plan can be like selecting the right tools for your jungle expedition. You must consider your needs, health conditions, and budget to find the best fit.

Don't be afraid to shop around, compare plans, and ask questions. You can also seek guidance from Medicare counselors or trusted advisors to help you make informed decisions.

Another strategy is to **consider long-term care insurance**. As we age, the risk of needing long-term care services, like assisted living or nursing home care, increases. These services can be expensive and can quickly deplete your retirement savings without proper planning.

Long-term care insurance is like a safety net if you encounter unexpected health challenges that require extended care. It can help cover the costs of these services, protect your assets, and provide peace of mind.

However, long-term care insurance can be complex and expensive, so it's essential to understand the options and choose a plan that fits your needs and budget.

And here's a pro tip: **don't underestimate the power of healthy habits**. Maintaining a healthy lifestyle can go a long way in reducing healthcare costs in retirement.

Regular exercise, a balanced diet, and stress management techniques can help you stay healthy, prevent chronic diseases, and reduce the need for expensive medical treatments.

It's like building a robust immune system to fight off potential health threats. You're investing in your long-term health and financial security by taking care of your physical and mental well-being.

And remember, managing healthcare costs in retirement is an ongoing journey, not a one-time event. It's about being proactive, informed, and adaptable, just like a seasoned explorer who navigates the jungle with caution, preparedness, and a sense of adventure.

By managing healthcare costs, you can protect your financial well-being and enjoy a fulfilling retirement without the constant worry of unexpected medical expenses. It's about controlling your health and finances and creating a roadmap to a secure and healthy future.

Part 4
Special Considerations for Veterans

Chapter 10
Social Security Benefits for Veterans

For those who have served our country, navigating the world of Social Security benefits can feel like maneuvering through a complex military operation with rules and regulations that seem like classified information. But fear not, veterans, for we're about to decode the eligibility requirements and equip you with the knowledge you need to secure your rightful benefits.

First and foremost, it's essential to understand that veterans are not automatically entitled to Social Security benefits simply because of their military service. Like all other citizens, veterans must meet specific eligibility criteria to qualify for these benefits. Think of it as a mission with specific objectives that must be met to achieve success.

The cornerstone of Social Security eligibility is work credits. These are earned through employment in jobs covered by Social Security. For every $1,640 you earn in 2025, you receive one credit, up to a maximum of four credits per year.

Now, here's where things get enjoyable for veterans. Military service can count towards those work credits! For every $300 earned in military pay before 1957, you receive one credit. And for active duty service from 1957 through 2001, you automatically receive credits for each service quarter.

It's like earning extra points for your dedication and service to our country. These military service credits can be a valuable boost, especially for veterans with gaps in their civilian work history due to deployments or other military obligations.

But it's not just about work credits. You must also meet certain age and citizenship requirements to qualify for Social Security benefits. To receive retirement benefits, you must be 62 years old and a U.S. citizen or lawful permanent resident.

Think of it like reaching a certain rank in the military before you're eligible for specific privileges or assignments. Similarly, with Social Security, reaching 62 is a crucial critical stone that unlocks your eligibility for retirement benefits.

Here's where things get more nuanced. The amount of your Social Security benefits depends on your average lifetime earnings. The more you've earned throughout your working years, the higher your benefits will be.

For veterans, this calculation includes both civilian earnings and military pay. It's like combining combat experience with civilian skills to achieve a higher rank in the retirement benefits hierarchy.

But it's not just about the amount of your earnings. The timing of your earnings also matters. Social Security calculates your benefits based on your highest 35 years of earnings. So, if you had some lower-earning years, perhaps during your early military career or while transitioning back to civilian life, those years might not be included in the calculation.

It's like focusing on your most successful missions when evaluating your military career. Similarly, with Social Security, the focus is on your highest-earning years to determine your benefit amount.

Now, here's an important point: if you're a veteran with a disability, you might also be eligible for Social Security disability benefits. These benefits are designed to provide financial support if you're unable to work due to a severe medical condition.

To qualify for disability benefits, you must meet the exact work credit requirements as retirement benefits. But you also need to provide medical evidence documenting your disability and its impact on your ability to work.

Think of it like receiving a Purple Heart for injuries sustained in combat. Disability benefits recognize the sacrifices you've made and the challenges you face due to your service-related condition.

And here's another important consideration: if you're a veteran receiving VA disability benefits, those benefits might affect your Social Security eligibility. The good news is that you can receive both VA disability and Social Security benefits, but there are some coordination rules to remember.

It's like receiving commendations from different branches of the military. Each commendation recognizes your service and contributions, but there might be some overlap or coordination required to ensure you're receiving the maximum benefits you're entitled to.

Navigating the world of Social Security benefits for veterans can be complex, but it's a crucial mission for securing your financial well-being in retirement. By understanding the eligibility requirements, coordinating your benefits, and seeking guidance when needed, you can ensure that your service and sacrifices are rewarded with the financial security you deserve.

10.2 Coordinating Social Security with VA Benefits

For those who have served our country, navigating the world of retirement benefits can feel like maneuvering through a complex military operation. There are different branches, specialized programs, and many acronyms to decipher. But fear not, veterans, for we're here to simplify the mission and help you coordinate your Social Security benefits with your well-deserved VA benefits.

Think of it like this: you're a skilled strategist planning a multi-pronged approach to secure your financial future in retirement. Social Security and VA benefits are like your two leading battalions, each with its strengths and capabilities. By coordinating their efforts strategically, you can maximize your resources and achieve your retirement goals more efficiently.

Social Security, as discussed throughout this book, is like your reliable infantry, providing a steady stream of income to cover your basic needs in retirement. It's the foundation of your retirement plan, the bedrock upon which you can build a secure and fulfilling future.

VA benefits, on the other hand, are like your specialized units, offering targeted support for specific needs, such as healthcare, disability compensation, and education assistance. They're designed to address the unique challenges veterans face, providing a safety net and opportunities for growth and well-being.

Here's the key to success: understanding how these two battalions can work together harmoniously. It's like coordinating a joint operation, ensuring that each unit plays its role effectively and their efforts complement each other.

One important aspect of coordination is **understanding the eligibility requirements for both programs**. As you know, Social Security is based on your work history and earnings. The more you've paid into the system, the higher your benefits will be.

VA benefits, on the other hand, are based on your military service and any service-connected disabilities you may have. The length of your service, rank, and the severity of your disabilities all factor into your eligibility for various VA programs.

It's like knowing the terrain of your battlefield. You need to understand each unit's strengths and limitations to deploy them effectively.

Another crucial aspect is **timing your benefit claims strategically**. You can claim Social Security as early as age 62, but your benefits will be reduced if you claim before your full retirement age (FRA). You can also delay claiming until age 70 to increase your monthly payments.

Similarly, VA benefits might have different eligibility ages and claiming options depending on the specific program. For example, you might be eligible for VA disability compensation at any age if you have a service-connected disability. Still, you should wait until age 65 to receive VA healthcare benefits.

Coordinating your claiming strategies can be like planning a synchronized attack. You want to time your moves carefully to maximize your benefits and ensure a steady income stream throughout your retirement.

For example, suppose you have a service-connected disability that qualifies you for VA disability compensation. In that case, consider claiming those benefits early to supplement your income while delaying your Social Security, claiming to increase your monthly payments later.

Or, if you're in good health and expect to live a long life, you may delay both your Social Security and VA benefit claims to maximize your lifetime income.

It's like choosing the right weapons for your arsenal. You want to select the tools that best suit your needs and circumstances to achieve your objectives.

Another important aspect of coordination is **understanding how different benefits affect each other**. For example, receiving VA disability compensation might affect your eligibility for Social Security disability benefits.

This is because both programs have similar eligibility criteria, and receiving benefits from one program might reduce the amount you're eligible for from the other.

It's like navigating a minefield. You must be aware of potential conflicts and take careful steps to avoid unintended consequences.

That's why it's crucial to **seek guidance from knowledgeable sources**. The Social Security Administration (SSA) and the Department of Veterans Affairs (VA) offer resources and assistance to help veterans understand their benefits and coordinate their claims.

You can also consult with a financial advisor or a veterans' benefits specialist who can provide personalized guidance and help you navigate the complexities of both programs.

Think of them as your trusted advisors, guiding you through the battlefield and helping you make strategic decisions that align with your retirement goals.

Coordinating your Social Security and VA benefits is like conducting a well-orchestrated symphony. Each instrument plays its part, creating a harmonious blend of sounds that resonate with your financial well-being.

By understanding the nuances of each program, timing your claims strategically, and seeking expert guidance, you can create a retirement plan that honors your service and provides a secure and fulfilling future.

10.3 Special Considerations for Disabled Veterans

Navigating the world of Social Security can present unique challenges and opportunities for those who have served our country. It's like embarking on a mission with a unique set of skills and experiences, requiring a tailored approach to ensure you receive the benefits you deserve.

Disabled veterans, in particular, face specific considerations regarding Social Security. Their service-related disabilities might impact their ability to work and earn income, making Social Security a crucial lifeline for their financial well-being.

It's like returning from a challenging deployment with valuable skills and carrying the weight of injuries or disabilities. Social Security is there to support and recognize those sacrifices, ensuring that disabled veterans have a safety net to rely on.

One important consideration is the **interaction between Social Security and VA disability benefits**. You might be wondering, "Can I receive both?" The answer is yes, but there are some nuances to understand.

Think of it like receiving two medals for your service, each recognizing a different aspect of your contribution. Social Security Disability benefits are based on your work history and contributions to the system, while VA disability benefits are based on your service-connected disabilities.

Both programs provide financial support but have different eligibility criteria and payment structures. Understanding how they interact and coordinate your applications is essential to maximize your benefits.

For example, if you're receiving VA disability benefits, those payments might reduce the amount of Social Security Disability benefits you're eligible for. But don't worry, this doesn't mean you'll lose out on benefits altogether. The SSA has a formula to ensure that you receive fair and equitable support from both programs.

It's like having two streams flowing into a single river. Each stream contributes to the overall flow, but the amount from each source might vary depending on the terrain and rainfall. Similarly, with Social Security and VA disability benefits, both programs contribute to your financial well-being, but the amount from each might vary depending on your circumstances.

Another consideration is the **impact of your disability rating on your Social Security benefits**. The Department of Veterans Affairs assigns disability ratings to veterans based on the severity of their service-connected disabilities. These ratings range from 0% to 100%, with higher ratings indicating more severe disabilities.

Your disability rating can affect your eligibility for Social Security Disability benefits and the amount you receive. For example, suppose you have a 100% disability rating from the VA. In that case, you might automatically qualify for Social Security Disability benefits, even if you haven't worked enough to earn the required credits.

It's like receiving a special commendation for your service, recognizing the significant impact your disability has on your ability to work and earn income. Social Security considers this, providing expedited access to benefits and ensuring you receive the support you need.

Another important factor is your **age and work history**. If you're a younger veteran with a limited work history, you might face challenges qualifying for Social Security Disability benefits based on your work credits alone. However, your service-connected disability can play a crucial role in your eligibility.

Think of it like this: your military service is like a unique training program that equips you with valuable skills and experience. Even if you haven't had a long civilian career, your service can be considered when evaluating your eligibility for Social Security Disability benefits.

It's like recognizing that your military experience has prepared you for the workforce, even if your disability prevents you from pursuing certain types of employment.

And here's a crucial point: **don't navigate this journey alone**. The world of Social Security and VA benefits can be complex, especially for disabled veterans. Seek guidance from veterans' organizations, Social Security specialists, and financial advisors who understand your unique challenges.

They can help you understand your options, coordinate your applications, and maximize your benefits. It's like having a trusted comrade by your side, guiding you through the terrain and ensuring you receive the support you deserve.

And remember, your service and sacrifice are valued. Social Security is there to provide a safety net, ensuring you have the financial resources to live a fulfilling life, even in the face of challenges. It's a testament to the nation's commitment to supporting those who have served and protected our country.

Chapter 11
Types of Benefits Available for Families

When a veteran passes away, it's a time of immense grief and loss for their family. Amidst the emotional turmoil, there are also practical matters to attend to, including ensuring the family's financial well-being. Social Security provides a comforting embrace, offering a range of benefits to support the families of deceased veterans.

It's like a promise kept, a recognition that the veteran's service and sacrifice extended beyond their lifetime, leaving a legacy of support for their loved ones. These benefits are a lifeline for surviving spouses, children, and even dependent parents, helping them navigate the financial challenges that often accompany the loss of a loved one.

One of the primary benefits available is **survivor benefits for spouses**. These benefits are designed to provide a steady income stream for the surviving spouse, helping them maintain their standard of living and cover essential expenses.

Think of it as a continuation of the veteran's commitment to their family, ensuring their partner is taken care of even when they're no longer physically present. The survivor benefits a spouse can receive depend on the veteran's work record and the spouse's age.

If the surviving spouse waits until their full retirement age (FRA), they can receive 100% of the veteran's benefit. However, they can also claim benefits as early as age 60, although their payments will be reduced if they claim before their FRA.

It's like having a financial safety net, a way to cushion the impact of the loss and provide stability during a difficult transition. These benefits can help cover housing costs, groceries, medical expenses, and other essential needs, allowing the surviving spouse to focus on healing and rebuilding their life.

Another significant benefit is **the survival benefit for children**. If the veteran had children under 18 (or up to 19 if still in high school), those children may also be eligible for survivor benefits. These benefits cover the costs of education, living expenses, and other needs, ensuring that the children have the support they need to thrive.

It's like a legacy of care, a way for veterans to continue providing for their children even after they're gone. These benefits can help pay for college tuition, extracurricular activities, and other opportunities that might have been part of the veteran's dreams for their children.

And it's not just spouses and children who can benefit. In some cases, **dependent parents** of deceased veterans may also be eligible for survivor benefits. This can provide crucial support for aging parents who rely on the veteran for financial assistance.

It's like recognizing the family's interconnectedness, a way to honor the veteran's commitment to their parents and ensure their well-being. These benefits cover living expenses, medical costs, and other needs, providing a safety net for those who depend on the veteran.

Here's an important point: **eligibility for these benefits depends on various factors**, including the veteran's service record, the family member's relationship with the veteran, and their income and resources.

It's like navigating a complex maze, with different pathways leading to different outcomes. Understanding the eligibility criteria and gathering the necessary documentation is crucial to ensuring you receive the benefits you deserve.

The Social Security Administration (SSA) provides detailed information about survivor and dependent benefits on its website and through its local offices. You can also seek guidance from veterans' organizations and financial advisors who specialize in helping veterans and their families.

It's like having a guide to help you navigate the maze, providing directions and support. They can help you understand the rules, gather the necessary documentation, and make informed decisions about your benefits.

And remember, these benefits are not just about financial support. They're also a recognition of the sacrifices made by veterans and their families. They're a way to honor their service and ensure that their loved ones are cared for, even in the face of loss.

It's like a tribute to the veteran's legacy, a way to ensure that their memory lives on through the support and well-being of their family. By understanding these benefits and accessing the support available, you can honor the veteran's memory and build a secure future for your family.

11.2 Eligibility and Application Process

When a veteran passes away, their family members often face a whirlwind of emotions and challenges. Amidst the grief and adjustments, there's also the practical matter of navigating financial issues and ensuring their well-being. Social Security provides a crucial lifeline in these difficult times, offering survivor and dependent benefits to help families cope with the loss and maintain their financial stability.

Think of it as a safety net woven with threads of compassion and support, catching families when they need it most. These benefits are a testament to the nation's commitment to honoring the service and sacrifice of veterans and extending that support to their loved ones even after they're gone.

However, navigating the eligibility and application process for these benefits can sometimes feel like traversing a maze, with rules and requirements that might initially seem confusing. Fear not, for we're here to guide you through this process step by step, ensuring you understand the requirements and receive the support you deserve.

Eligibility:

First, let's talk about who's eligible for these benefits. Generally, the following family members of a deceased veteran may qualify:

- **Spouse:** A surviving spouse may be eligible for survivor benefits, whether married at the time of the veteran's death or divorced after at least 10 years of marriage. The amount they receive depends on the veteran's work record and the surviving spouse's age and earnings.
- **Children:** Unmarried children under 18 (or up to 19 if still in high school) may qualify for benefits. This also includes stepchildren, adopted children, and, in some cases, grandchildren who were dependent on the veteran.
- **Parents:** In certain circumstances, dependent parents of a deceased veteran may also be eligible for benefits.

Now, here's where things get a bit more nuanced. The eligibility criteria for survivor and dependent benefits can vary depending on the veteran's service history, disability status, and the specific circumstances of their death.

For example, if the veteran died due to a service-connected disability, their family members might be eligible for higher benefits or have different eligibility requirements.

It's like navigating a river with different currents and depths. You need to understand the specific characteristics of the river to steer your boat safely and reach your destination. Similarly, with survivor and dependent benefits, it's crucial to understand the particular rules and requirements that apply to your situation.

Application Process:

Now, let's discuss the application process. Although applying for survivor and dependent benefits might initially seem daunting, with the proper guidance and preparation, it can be a smooth and straightforward process.

The first step is to gather the necessary documents, including the veteran's death certificate, marriage certificate (if applicable), birth certificates of dependent children, and Social Security numbers for all applicants.

It's like packing your backpack for a hike, ensuring you have all the essential gear and supplies to navigate the terrain. Similarly, with the application process, having all the necessary documents on hand can make the journey smoother and more efficient.

You can apply for benefits online, by phone, or at a Social Security office. The SSA provides helpful resources and guidance on their website (ssa.gov), and you can also call their toll-free number to speak with a representative.

It's like having a map and a compass to guide you through the application process. The SSA provides the tools and support to navigate the terrain and reach your destination.

When you apply, the SSA will review your application and supporting documents to determine your eligibility. They might also request additional information or documentation, so it's essential to be responsive and provide any requested materials promptly.

It's like encountering a checkpoint along your journey. The SSA must verify your identity and eligibility before allowing you to proceed. You can ensure a smooth and timely process by providing the necessary information and cooperating with their requests.

Once your application is approved, you'll start receiving monthly benefits, which can provide a crucial financial lifeline for your family during a challenging time. These benefits cover living expenses, pay for education, and give security as you adjust to your new reality.

It's like reaching a haven after a long journey. The survivor and dependent benefits provide comfort and stability, allowing you to focus on healing and rebuilding your life.

And remember, you're not alone on this journey. The SSA, veterans' organizations, and financial advisors are there to provide support and guidance along the way. They can help you understand the rules, navigate the application process, and maximize your benefits.

It's like having a team of experienced guides, ensuring you reach your destination safely and receive the support you deserve. By understanding the eligibility criteria, gathering the necessary documents, and seeking guidance when needed, you can navigate the application process with confidence and ensure that your family receives the financial support they need to honor the legacy of your loved one and build a secure future.

11.3 Planning for the Financial Security of Your Family

When you've dedicated your life to serving your country, ensuring the financial security of your loved ones becomes a top priority. It's like building a sturdy fortress to protect your family from life's uncertainties, a legacy of care and support that extends beyond your lifetime.

For veterans and their families, Social Security survivor and dependent benefits play a crucial role in this fortress, providing a safety net in the event of unexpected circumstances. It's like having a backup plan and a reserve unit ready to step in and provide support when it's needed most.

However, navigating these benefits can be like maneuvering through a complex battlefield, requiring careful planning and strategic decision-making. It's about understanding the terrain, anticipating potential challenges, and equipping your family with the knowledge and resources they need to thrive.

One crucial step is to **understand the different types of benefits available**. Social Security offers a range of survivor and dependent benefits for veterans' families, each with its own eligibility criteria and payment structure.

Think of it as assembling a team of specialists, each with unique skills and expertise. Benefits are available for spouses, children, and even dependent parents, each designed to provide support in specific situations.

For example, a surviving spouse might be eligible for monthly payments based on the veteran's work record. At the same time, a dependent child might receive benefits to help cover education and living expenses. It's about understanding which benefits your family might qualify for and how to access them when the time comes.

Another critical step is to **coordinate your Social Security benefits with other sources of income and support**. Many veterans also receive benefits from the Department of Veterans Affairs (VA), such as disability compensation or pension payments.

It's like having multiple supply lines to your fortress, ensuring that your family has access to resources from different sources. However, coordinating these benefits can be complex and requires careful planning and communication with both the SSA and the VA.

For example, if you're receiving VA disability benefits, those payments might reduce the amount of Social Security survivor benefits your family is eligible for. But don't worry, this doesn't mean your family will lose out on benefits altogether. The SSA has a formula to ensure that your family receives a fair and equitable amount of support from both programs.

It's like having two streams flowing into a single river. Each stream contributes to the overall flow, but the amount from each source might vary depending on the terrain and rainfall. Similarly, with Social Security and VA benefits, both programs contribute to your family's financial well-being, but the amount from each might vary depending on your circumstances.

Another crucial aspect of planning is to **consider your family's long-term financial needs**. Retirement planning isn't just about covering immediate expenses; it's about ensuring your family's financial security for years to come.

Think of it like building a sustainable fortress, one that can withstand the test of time and provide shelter for generations to come. This might involve creating a budget, saving for future expenses, and investing wisely to grow your assets.

If you have young children, consider setting up a college fund or investing in a life insurance policy to provide for their education and future needs. If you have a spouse who relies on your income, you should ensure they have access to adequate retirement savings and survivor benefits.

It's about creating a financial roadmap that guides your family towards a secure and fulfilling future, even in your absence.

And here's a crucial point: **communication is vital**. Talk to your family about your financial plans, explain the benefits they might be eligible for, and ensure they understand how to access those benefits when the time comes.

It's like briefing your troops before a mission, ensuring everyone understands their roles and responsibilities. Empower your family with knowledge and information so they can navigate the complexities of Social Security and VA benefits with confidence.

You can also seek guidance from veterans' organizations, financial advisors, and Social Security specialists who can provide personalized advice and support. It's like having a team of experienced advisors by your side, helping you develop a comprehensive plan that meets your family's unique needs.

Remember, planning for your family's financial security is an act of love and responsibility. It's about providing a legacy of support and ensuring that your loved ones have the resources they need to thrive, even in the face of life's uncertainties.

By understanding the benefits available, coordinating your resources, and communicating with your family, you can build a solid financial foundation that will protect and support them for generations to come. It's like leaving behind a well-equipped fortress, a symbol of your love and commitment to their well-being.

Part 5
Resources and Next Steps

Chapter 12
Online Resources and Tools for Social Security Planning

In today's digital age, information is at our fingertips, and when it comes to Social Security, the Social Security Administration (SSA) website is a treasure trove of valuable resources. It's like having a personal Social Security encyclopedia, a comprehensive guide to navigating the intricacies of the program and planning for your retirement.

You might be thinking, "Government websites? Aren't they usually boring and difficult to navigatc?" The SSA website has undergone a significant transformation in recent years, becoming a user-friendly hub of information, tools, and resources for people of all ages.

Think of it like a modern library, with well-organized shelves, helpful librarians, and a cozy reading corner where you can delve into the topics that interest you most. The SSA website offers a wealth of information on everything from eligibility requirements and benefit calculations to claiming strategies and online services.

One of the website's most valuable features is your **personal "My Social Security" account**. It's like having a personalized Social Security dashboard, a secure online space where you can access your earnings history, estimate your future benefits, and even manage your payments.

You can track your earnings throughout your career, see how much you've contributed to Social Security, and get a clear picture of your future benefits. It's like having a financial crystal ball, allowing you to peek into the future and plan for your retirement with greater confidence.

And here's the best part: you can access your "My Social Security" account from anywhere with an internet connection. Whether you're at home, at the library, or even on vacation, you can stay connected to your Social Security information and manage your benefits with ease.

Another valuable resource on the website is the **Retirement Estimator**. It's like having a personal financial calculator, allowing you to estimate your future benefits based on your earnings history and projected retirement age.

You can play around with different scenarios, see how delaying your claim might affect your monthly payments, and get a clearer picture of your retirement income options. It's like having a financial playground where you can explore different possibilities and make informed decisions about your future.

And if you're curious about how the 2025 COLA might affect your benefits, the website has you covered. You can find detailed information about the COLA calculation, historical trends, and projections for the future. It's like having a direct line to the economic forecasters, keeping you informed about the factors that might impact your retirement income.

The SSA website also offers a wealth of **educational resources**, such as articles, blog posts, and even videos that explain Social Security in plain language. It's like having a personal tutor guiding you through the program's complexities and answering your questions clearly and concisely.

You can learn about different types of benefits, eligibility requirements, claiming strategies, and even how to coordinate your Social Security with other sources of income. It's like having a comprehensive guidebook to retirement planning, all in one convenient location.

If you prefer a more interactive learning experience, the website offers **online seminars and webinars** on various Social Security topics. It's like attending a virtual classroom, where you can learn from experts, ask questions, and connect with other people who are planning for their retirement.

These seminars cover a wide range of topics, from understanding your benefits and claiming strategies to managing your finances and planning for healthcare costs in retirement. It's like having a personal retirement coach guiding you through the process and providing valuable insights and advice.

If you're looking for a more personalized experience, the website offers a **"Contact Us" feature** where you can reach out to SSA representatives with your questions or concerns. It's like having a direct line to Social Security experts ready to assist you with any issues you might encounter.

Whether you have questions about your benefits, need help with your online account, or want to schedule an appointment at a local office, the SSA website provides a convenient way to connect with the resources you need.

The SSA website is a dynamic and evolving resource, constantly updated with the latest information and tools to help you navigate the world of Social Security. It's like having a trusted companion on your retirement journey, providing guidance, support, and a wealth of information to help you achieve your financial goals.

By exploring the website's features, utilizing its tools, and accessing its educational resources, you can become an informed and empowered Social Security beneficiary, ready to make the most of your retirement years. It's like having a key to unlock the treasures of Social Security, opening up a world of possibilities for a secure and fulfilling future.

12.2 Retirement Planning Calculators and Tools

In today's digital age, planning for retirement is like embarking on a high-tech expedition equipped with powerful tools and resources to guide you through the financial wilderness. And just like a seasoned explorer would rely on their compass, maps, and GPS to navigate unfamiliar terrain, you can leverage online retirement planning calculators and tools to chart your course towards a secure and fulfilling retirement.

These online resources are like virtual assistants, providing valuable insights, crunching numbers, and offering personalized guidance to help you make informed decisions about your financial future. They can help you estimate your retirement income needs, project your Social Security benefits, and even explore different investment strategies.

One of the most valuable tools is the **Social Security Administration's Retirement Estimator**. It's like a personalized crystal ball that provides estimates of your future Social Security benefits based on your actual earnings record.

You simply enter some basic information, like your birth date and estimated future earnings, and the estimator generates a projection of your monthly benefits at different claiming ages. It's like getting a sneak peek into your retirement income, allowing you to plan and make adjustments as needed.

Another helpful tool is the **AARP Retirement Calculator**. This comprehensive calculator takes a broader approach, considering not just

Social Security but also other income sources, like pensions and retirement savings.

You can input your current savings, estimated expenses, and desired retirement lifestyle, and the calculator will provide a personalized roadmap, showing you whether you're on track to meet your goals or need to make adjustments.

It's like having a financial GPS that guides you toward your retirement destination, providing turn-by-turn directions and alerts if you veer off course.

For those who prefer a more visual approach, there are **interactive retirement planning tools** that use graphs and charts to illustrate their financial journey. These tools can help them visualize their progress, track their savings, and see the impact of different investment strategies on their retirement income.

It's like having a 3D map of your retirement landscape, allowing you to explore different paths and choose the one that best suits your needs and goals.

Many financial websites and institutions also offer **specialized calculators** that focus on specific aspects of retirement planning. For example, some calculators can help you estimate your healthcare costs in retirement, project your life expectancy, or even determine how much you need to save to maintain your current lifestyle.

It's like having a toolbox filled with specialized gadgets for different tasks. You can choose the tool that best suits your needs and use it to fine-tune your retirement plan.

And here's a pro tip: **don't rely solely on online calculators and tools**. While they can provide valuable insights and guidance, they're not a substitute for professional financial advice.

Think of them as helpful assistants but not the ultimate decision-makers. It's always wise to consult with a qualified financial advisor who can assess your circumstances, understand your goals, and provide personalized recommendations.

They can help you navigate the complexities of retirement planning, choose the right investment strategies, and ensure your financial plan is aligned with your overall life goals.

Remember, the world of online retirement planning tools is constantly evolving. New calculators and resources are continually being developed, offering even more sophisticated and personalized guidance.

It's like having access to the latest and greatest navigation technology, constantly updating your maps, and providing real-time information to help you stay on course.

By staying informed, exploring different tools, and seeking professional advice when needed, you can leverage the power of online resources to create a comprehensive and resilient retirement plan. It's about empowering yourself with knowledge, taking control of your financial future, and navigating your retirement journey with confidence and clarity.

12.3 Finding Reputable Financial Advice Online

Navigating the vast ocean of online financial advice can feel like sailing through uncharted waters, with hidden reefs and treacherous currents lurking beneath the surface. But fear not, fellow navigator, for with the right tools and a discerning eye, you can chart a safe course and discover valuable resources to guide your retirement journey.

The internet is a treasure trove of information, offering a wealth of knowledge at your fingertips. But it's also a breeding ground for misinformation, with unreliable sources and self-proclaimed experts vying for your attention.

It's like exploring a bustling marketplace filled with vendors selling all sorts of goods, some genuine and valuable, others counterfeit and deceptive. You need to be a savvy shopper, discerning the natural treasures from the cheap imitations.

When seeking financial advice online, it's crucial to **start with trusted sources**. Think of these as your reliable beacons, guiding you towards safe harbors in the vast online sea.

The Social Security Administration (SSA) website, ssa.gov, is your official port of call for all things Social Security. It's like the government's flagship, carrying a wealth of information about benefits, eligibility, and claiming strategies.

You can find your personalized Social Security statement, estimate your future benefits, and even apply for benefits online. It's like having a direct line to the captain of the ship, ensuring you have the most accurate and up-to-date information.

Another trusted source is the **Department of Labor** website, dol.gov. It offers a wealth of information about retirement planning, including investment options, pension plans, and workplace savings programs.

It's like having a seasoned navigator by your side, providing guidance and support as you chart your retirement course.

Remember **reputable financial publications** like KKiplinger, The Motley Fool, and Forbes. These publications offer articles, reports, and analyses from experienced financial journalists and experts, providing valuable insights and perspectives on retirement planning.

It's like having access to a library of nautical charts, providing detailed maps and information to help you navigate the financial waters.

But here's a crucial point: **not all online sources are created equal**. Just because a website looks professional or claims to offer expert advice doesn't mean it's reliable.

It's like encountering a siren song luring you towards treacherous rocks. You need to be wary of websites that promote specific products or services, offer unrealistic promises, or lack transparency about their sources and credentials.

When evaluating online financial advice, **consider the source's credibility**. Are you affiliated with a reputable organization or institution? Do they have relevant credentials or experience in the field? Are they transparent about their potential biases or conflicts of interest?

It's like checking the captain's credentials before boarding a ship. You want to ensure they have the experience and expertise to navigate safely and responsibly.

Another critical factor is **the quality of the information**. Is it accurate, up-to-date, and supported by evidence? Does it align with your values and financial goals? Does it provide practical advice that you can implement in your own life?

It's like examining the nautical charts for accuracy and relevance. You want to ensure they reflect the current conditions and guide you towards your desired destination.

And don't forget about **your gut feeling**. If something seems too good to be true or makes you feel uncomfortable, trust your instincts. There are plenty of other reputable sources out there, so don't feel pressured to follow advice that doesn't resonate with you.

It's like listening to the whispers of the wind and the currents, sensing potential dangers, and adjusting your course accordingly.

Now, here's a pro tip: **be wary of social media and online forums**. While these platforms can be great for connecting with others and sharing experiences, they're also breeding grounds for misinformation and unqualified advice.

It's like listening to rumors and gossip at a crowded port. While some stories might be entertaining, they're not always reliable or trustworthy.

Always verify information from social media or online forums with trusted sources before making any financial decisions. It's like double-checking your nautical charts with a seasoned navigator before setting sail.

And remember, finding reputable financial advice online is an ongoing journey, not a one-time event. It's about staying vigilant, discerning, and informed, just like a skilled navigator who constantly scans the horizon for potential hazards and adjusts their course accordingly.

By using trusted sources, evaluating credibility, and trusting your instincts, you can navigate the online world with confidence and discover valuable resources to guide your retirement planning. It's about charting a safe and successful course, ensuring your financial ship reaches its destination with your dreams and aspirations intact.

Chapter 13
Choosing a Qualified Financial Advisor

Embarking on the retirement planning journey can sometimes feel like setting sail on a vast ocean, with uncharted waters and unpredictable currents ahead. While you've already equipped yourself with valuable knowledge about Social Security and COLA, there might be times when you need the guidance of an experienced navigator or a trusted financial advisor to help you chart the best course.

Think of a financial advisor as your co-captain, someone who understands the intricacies of the financial seas and can help you navigate towards your retirement goals. They can provide personalized advice, answer your questions, and offer support as you make important decisions about your financial future.

But just like choosing a crew for your voyage, selecting a qualified financial advisor is a crucial decision that requires careful consideration. You want someone trustworthy, experienced, and aligned with your values and goals.

It's like finding a skilled and reliable first mate, someone you can trust to guide the ship and keep you on course, even in stormy weather.

One crucial factor to consider is the **advisor's credentials and experience**. Just like you'd want a captain with years of experience navigating the seas, you want a financial advisor with a proven track record and relevant expertise.

Look for advisors who hold certifications like Certified Financial Planner (CFP), Chartered Financial Analyst (CFA), or Chartered Financial Consultant (ChFC). These certifications indicate that the advisor has met rigorous education and experience requirements and adheres to ethical standards.

It's like checking the captain's certifications and licenses before setting sail. You want to ensure they have the necessary qualifications and knowledge to navigate safely and responsibly.

Another critical factor is the **advisor's fiduciary duty**. A fiduciary is legally obligated to act in your best interest, putting your needs ahead of their own. That is crucial when seeking financial advice, as it ensures that the advisor is working for you, not for their profit.

Think of it as having a loyal first mate who always prioritizes the ship's and crew's safety, even if it means sacrificing their comfort or gain.

When interviewing potential advisors, ask them directly if they are fiduciaries and whether they adhere to a fiduciary standard in all their client relationships. It's like asking the captain to swear an oath of loyalty and commitment to your voyage.

Another crucial aspect is the **advisor's communication style and approach**. You want someone who listens to your concerns, understands your goals, and explains complex financial concepts clearly and understandably.

It's like having a captain who effectively communicates with the crew, explains the navigation plan, addresses concerns, and fosters a sense of trust and collaboration.

When meeting with potential advisors, pay attention to how they interact with you. Do they listen attentively? Do they answer your questions thoroughly? Do they make you feel comfortable and understood?

It's like assessing the captain's communication skills before setting sail. You want someone who can clearly explain the journey ahead, address your concerns, and keep you informed along the way.

Another important consideration is the **advisor's fees and compensation structure**. Financial advisors typically charge fees for their services, which can vary depending on their experience, expertise, and the type of services they provide.

Some advisors charge a flat fee, while others charge a percentage of your assets under management. Some might even receive commissions for selling certain financial products.

It's like understanding the cost of hiring a crew for your voyage. You want to ensure the fees are transparent, reasonable, and aligned with the value you receive.

When discussing fees with potential advisors, ask for a clear breakdown of their charges and how they are calculated. Don't hesitate to negotiate fees or compare different advisors to find the best value for your needs.

And here's a pro tip: **don't be afraid to ask for referrals**. Talk to friends, family members, or colleagues who have worked with financial advisors and ask for their recommendations.

It's like getting recommendations from fellow sailors who have navigated similar waters. They can share their experiences, offer insights, and help you find a qualified advisor who meets your needs.

You can also use online resources, like the CFP Board website or the National Association of Personal Financial Advisors (NAPFA) website, to find certified financial planners in your area. These websites provide directories of qualified advisors and allow you to filter your search based on your location, specialization, and other criteria.

It's like having access to a map of experienced navigators, helping you find the right guide for your financial journey.

Choosing a qualified financial advisor is a crucial step in your retirement planning journey. It's about finding a trusted partner who can help you navigate the complexities of the financial world and achieve your retirement goals.

By considering the advisor's credentials, fiduciary duty, communication style, fees, and referrals, you can make an informed decision and find a co-captain who will guide you toward a secure and fulfilling retirement.

13.2 Questions to Ask Your Advisor

Think of finding the right financial advisor as like choosing a trusted guide for a challenging mountain climb. You wouldn't just pick someone at random, would you? You'd want someone experienced, knowledgeable, and who understands your individual needs and goals.

Similarly, when seeking professional guidance for your retirement planning, it's crucial to ask the right questions to ensure you're finding an advisor who is a good fit for you. It's about having a conversation, not just a sales pitch, and making sure your advisor is genuinely invested in your financial well-being.

One of the first questions to ask is about their **credentials and experience**. What certifications do they hold? How long have they been working with clients like you? What is their area of expertise?

It's like checking the guide's climbing resume. You want to know that you have conquered similar peaks before and have the skills and experience to guide you safely to the summit.

Don't hesitate to ask about their education, professional affiliations, and any specialized training they've received in retirement planning or

Social Security. It's about ensuring they have the knowledge and expertise to navigate the complexities of your financial landscape.

Another critical question is about their **approach to financial planning**. What is their philosophy? How do they tailor their advice to individual clients? What strategies do they typically recommend?

It's like understanding the guide's climbing style. Do you prefer a steady and cautious approach, or are you more adventurous and risk-taking? You want to make sure their style aligns with your preferences and risk tolerance.

Ask about their investment philosophy, their approach to retirement income planning, and how they incorporate Social Security and other benefits into their recommendations. It's about finding an advisor who understands your vision for retirement and can help you chart a course that aligns with your values and goals.

A crucial question to ask is about their **fees and compensation**. How do they charge for their services? Do they charge a flat fee, an hourly rate, or a percentage of your assets under management? Are there any hidden fees or commissions?

It's like understanding the cost of the expedition upfront. You want to know what you're paying for and ensure the fees are transparent and reasonable.

Don't be afraid to ask for a detailed breakdown of their fees and compare them with other advisors. It's about making an informed decision and ensuring you're getting value for your investment.

Another critical question is about their **fiduciary responsibility**. A fiduciary is legally obligated to act in your best interest, putting your needs ahead of their own.

It's like having a guide who is genuinely committed to your safety and success, not just your gain.

Ask your advisor if they are a fiduciary and whether they adhere to a fiduciary standard in all their interactions with you. That ensures they are ethically bound to provide advice that is in your best interest, not just what's most profitable for them.

You can also ask about their **approach to communication and client relationships**. How often will you meet with them? How do they provide updates and reports? Are they available to answer your questions and address your concerns?

It's like establishing a clear communication protocol for your climb. You want to know how often you'll check in with your guide, how to keep you informed about the journey, and whether you will be available to answer your questions and address your concerns along the way.

A good advisor will be responsive, communicative, and proactive in keeping you informed about your financial progress. It's about building a relationship of trust and transparency, where you feel comfortable sharing your financial concerns and aspirations.

Remember to ask about their **experience with Social Security and COLA**. Do they have a deep understanding of these topics? Can they provide guidance on claiming strategies, coordinating benefits with other income sources, and planning for the impact of COLA adjustments?

It's like ensuring your guide has experience navigating the specific terrain of your chosen mountain. You want them to be familiar with the challenges and opportunities that lie ahead and provide expert guidance to help you reach your summit.

Finally, ask about their **approach to retirement planning beyond investments**. Do they consider other aspects of your financial well-being, such as healthcare costs, housing expenses, and potential long-term care needs?

It's like ensuring your guide has a holistic view of the expedition, not just focusing on the climb itself. You want to consider all aspects of your journey, including your physical and mental well-being, to ensure a safe and successful experience.

By asking these questions and engaging in a thoughtful conversation, you can find a financial advisor who is a true partner in your retirement journey. It's about building a relationship of trust, transparency, and shared goals, ensuring that you have the guidance and support you need to navigate the complexities of retirement planning and achieve your financial aspirations.

13.3 Working with a Financial Planner to Achieve Your Goals

Think of a financial planner as your experienced Sherpa guiding you on your climb towards the summit of retirement. They've navigated these treacherous slopes before, they know the best paths to take, and they can help you avoid hidden crevasses and unexpected storms.

While this book provides you with a wealth of knowledge about Social Security, COLA, and other retirement essentials, sometimes you need a personalized touch guide who can assess your unique situation and create a customized plan to help you reach your specific goals.

That's where a financial planner comes in. They're like your financial personal trainers, helping you develop a tailored workout routine to achieve your desired fitness level. They can help you assess your current financial health, identify your strengths and weaknesses, and create a plan that aligns with your individual needs and aspirations.

However, working with a financial planner is not just about receiving a cookie-cutter plan. It's about building a collaborative relationship, a partnership where you and your planner work together to achieve your shared vision of retirement.

It's like embarking on a challenging hike with a trusted companion. You share the journey, support each other along the way, and celebrate the victories together.

One key benefit of working with a financial planner is their ability to **provide a holistic perspective**. They don't just focus on one aspect of your finances, like investments or Social Security. They consider the whole picture, including your income, expenses, assets, debts, and even your values and goals.

It's like having a panoramic view of the mountain range and understanding the interconnectedness of different peaks and valleys. A financial planner can help you see the big picture and make informed decisions that align with your overall economic well-being.

They can also help you **develop a comprehensive retirement plan**. This includes not just determining how much money you need to save but also creating a strategy for withdrawing those savings, managing your investments, and navigating Social Security and other income sources.

It's like having a detailed map of your climbing route, outlining the best paths to take, potential challenges to anticipate, and milestones to celebrate along the way.

A financial planner can also help you **stay on track and adjust your plan as needed**. Life is full of surprises, and your retirement journey might not always follow the initial plan. Unexpected expenses, health challenges, or changes in your circumstances can throw you off course.

But with a financial planner by your side, you have a trusted guide to help you navigate those detours and adjust your plan accordingly. It's like having a seasoned Sherpa who can adapt to changing weather conditions and guide you safely through unexpected obstacles.

They can also help you **make informed decisions about Social Security**. As we've discussed throughout this book, Social Security can be complex, with various claiming strategies and rules to consider.

A financial planner can help you understand your options, analyze the pros and cons of different claiming strategies, and make the best decision for your circumstances. It's like having a knowledgeable guide who can decipher the ancient maps and lead you to the hidden treasure of Social Security benefits.

They can also help you **manage your investments**. Investing can be intimidating, especially if you're not familiar with the financial markets. A financial planner can help you create a diversified portfolio, choose appropriate investments, and monitor your performance over time.

It's like having a skilled gardener tending to your retirement garden, ensuring that your investments are well-nourished and thriving.

And here's a crucial point: **working with a financial planner is not just for the wealthy**. Many financial planners offer services on a fee-only basis, meaning they charge a flat fee or an hourly rate for their services, regardless of your asset size.

That makes financial planning accessible to a broader range of individuals, including those with modest incomes or limited savings. It's like having access to an experienced guide, regardless of your climbing experience or the size of your backpack.

If you're considering working with a financial planner, **it's essential to find someone you trust and feel comfortable with**. Look for a planner who has relevant credentials, experience, and a fiduciary duty to act in your best interests.

It's like choosing a climbing partner who shares your values, understands your goals, and has the skills and experience to guide you safely.

You can also ask for referrals from friends, family, or trusted advisors. And don't hesitate to interview multiple planners before making a decision. It's like auditioning potential climbing partners, ensuring you find the right fit for your personality and goals.

By working with a financial planner, you're investing in your financial future, creating a partnership that can help you achieve your retirement dreams and navigate the complexities of Social Security and other financial matters. It's like having a trusted guide by your side, helping you climb the mountain of retirement with confidence and reach the summit with a sense of accomplishment and financial security.

Chapter 14
Staying Informed About Social Security Policy

Think of Social Security as a grand, ongoing conversation, a dialogue between policymakers, experts, and, most importantly, you – the beneficiaries. It's not a static program set in stone; it's constantly evolving, responding to economic shifts, demographic changes, and the voices of those it serves.

Staying informed about Social Security policy is like tuning into this conversation, understanding the issues at play, and making your voice heard. It's about being an active participant in shaping the future of this vital program, ensuring it remains a robust and reliable safety net for generations to come.

Now, you might be thinking, "Policy? Isn't that boring stuff for politicians and bureaucrats?" But trust me, Social Security policy has a real impact on your life, affecting your benefits, your retirement planning, and your overall financial well-being.

It's like checking the weather forecast before embarking on a long journey. You want to know if there are any storms brewing, potential detours to consider, or changes in the wind that affect your course.

Similarly, staying informed about Social Security policy allows you to anticipate potential changes, adjust your plans accordingly, and advocate for policies that protect your interests and ensure a secure retirement.

So, how do you stay informed? It's like tuning in to different channels on your radio, each offering a unique perspective and valuable information.

One channel is the **official Social Security Administration (SSA) website**, ssa.gov. It's like the government's newsroom, providing updates on policy changes, benefit adjustments, and program news.

You can sign up for email alerts, subscribe to their blog, and even follow them on social media to stay in the loop. It's like having a direct line to the policymakers, receiving firsthand information about the issues that affect your retirement.

Another channel is **reputable news sources**. Major media outlets, like The New York Times, The Wall Street Journal, and NPR, often report on Social Security policy, providing in-depth analysis and expert commentary.

It's like having a team of investigative reporters dig into the details, uncover hidden trends, and provide a broader context for understanding the issues.

And don't forget about **non-profit organizations** that advocate for seniors and retirement security, like AARP and The Senior Citizens League. They often publish reports, articles, and newsletters that provide valuable insights into Social Security policy and its potential impact on beneficiaries.

It's like having a group of experienced advisors by your side, offering guidance and support as you navigate the complexities of retirement planning.

However, staying informed is not just about passively consuming information. It's also about **actively engaging in the conversation**. Attend town hall meetings, write letters to your elected officials, and participate in online forums and discussions.

It's like joining a community of like-minded individuals, sharing your concerns, and collectively advocating for policies that protect your retirement security.

You can also support organizations that advocate for seniors and Social Security, donating your time or resources to help them amplify their message and influence policy decisions. It's like joining a grassroots movement, using your voice and actions to shape the future of retirement security.

And here's a crucial point: **don't underestimate the power of your voice**. Policymakers pay attention to public opinion, and your feedback can influence their decisions.

It's like casting your vote in the grand conversation of Social Security, making your voice heard, and shaping the direction of the program.

By staying informed, engaging in the conversation, and advocating for your interests, you become an active participant in shaping the future of Social Security, ensuring it remains a robust and reliable safety net for you and generations to come. It's about taking ownership of your retirement security, navigating the policy landscape with confidence, and ensuring your voice is heard in the ongoing dialogue about this vital program.

14.2 Making Your Voice Heard: Contacting Your Representatives

You've spent this entire book learning about the ins and outs of Social Security, COLA, and retirement planning. You're becoming the savvy navigator of your financial future! But here's the thing: your voice matters. You're not just a passenger on this retirement journey; you're an active participant, and you have the power to shape the course of Social Security and advocate for your retirement security.

Think of it like being part of a crew on a grand sailing expedition. You're not just along for the ride; you have a role to play, whether it's hoisting the sails, navigating the ship, or keeping watch for potential hazards. Similarly, when it comes to Social Security, your voice and your actions can make a difference.

One powerful way to make your voice heard is by contacting your elected representatives. They're like the ship's captains, responsible for steering the course of policy and legislation. By sharing your concerns, suggestions, and experiences, you can influence their decisions and help shape the future of Social Security.

You might be thinking, "But I'm just one person. What difference can I make?" Well, remember that a ship is steered by a collective effort, with each crew member contributing their skills and insights. Similarly, in the world of politics, your voice adds to a chorus of voices, amplifying the message and creating a wave of change.

When you contact your representatives, you're not just expressing your opinion; you're providing valuable feedback that can inform their decision-making. They need to hear from their constituents, understand their concerns, and learn about the real-life impact of policies on people's lives.

It's like sending a message in a bottle, sharing your experiences and observations with those who have the power to chart a better course.

Now, you might be wondering, "Who are my representatives, and how do I contact them?" Well, it's like identifying the key members of the ship's crew. You have your Senators, who represent your state at the federal level, and your Representatives, who represent your district in the House of Representatives.

You can find their contact information on the official websites of the Senate (senate.gov) and the House of Representatives (house.gov). It's like having a directory of the ship's crew, allowing you to connect with the right people and deliver your message effectively.

When contacting your representatives, it's essential to be clear, concise, and respectful. State your concerns, share your personal experiences, and offer suggestions for improvement. It's like presenting a well-crafted proposal to the ship's captain, outlining your ideas and recommendations for a better voyage.

You can also share relevant data and statistics to support your arguments. For example, mention the latest projections for the 2025 COLA, highlighting the potential impact on beneficiaries and the need for adjustments to ensure retirement security.

It's like presenting the captain with nautical charts and weather forecasts, providing evidence to support your proposed course correction.

Remember to personalize your message. Share your story, explain how Social Security has impacted your life, and express your hopes and concerns for the future. It's like sharing your logbook with the captain, providing a firsthand account of your journey and the challenges you've encountered.

Personal stories can be powerful tools for advocacy, creating empathy and understanding. They can help your representatives see the human impact of policies and inspire them to take action.

And here's a pro tip: **follow up with your representatives**. Don't just send a message and forget about it. Follow up with a phone call or another email to reiterate your concerns and inquire about their stance on the issue.

It's like checking in with the captain after presenting your proposal, ensuring that your message has been received and understood.

Advocacy is not a one-time event; it's an ongoing process that requires persistence and engagement. By staying informed, contacting your representatives, and sharing your voice, you can contribute to a more robust and more secure Social Security system for generations to come.

It's like being an active and engaged crew member, contributing your skills and insights to ensure a safe and successful voyage for everyone on board. Your voice matters, and your actions can make a difference in shaping the future of retirement security.

14.3 Joining Organizations that Support Retirement Security

Think of your retirement security as a grand tapestry woven with threads of savings, investments, Social Security benefits, and a dash of good fortune. But just like any intricate artwork, this tapestry needs support and reinforcement to withstand the test of time.

Joining organizations that champion retirement security is like adding a sturdy frame to your financial masterpiece. It's about connecting with like-minded individuals, amplifying your voice, and contributing to a collective effort to protect and enhance the retirement landscape for yourself and future generations.

These organizations are like vibrant communities of weavers, each contributing their unique skills and perspectives to create a stronger and more resilient tapestry. They advocate for policies that protect Social Security, promote retirement savings, and ensure a secure future for retirees.

They're like watch dogs guarding the integrity of your financial fortress, monitoring legislative changes, advocating for your rights, and providing valuable resources and information to help you navigate the retirement maze.

One such organization is AARP, formerly known as the American Association of Retired Persons. It's like a grand council of elders, representing the interests of millions of retirees and advocating for policies that enhance their quality of life.

AARP provides a wealth of resources, including information on Social Security, Medicare, retirement planning, and consumer protection. They also offer discounts on various products and services, helping you stretch your retirement budget further.

It's like having a wise mentor by your side, offering guidance, support, and a sense of community as you navigate the retirement journey.

Another valuable organization is the National Committee to Preserve Social Security and Medicare. They're like a dedicated task force, fiercely protecting the integrity of these vital programs and advocating for policies that strengthen their long-term sustainability.

They monitor legislative developments, educate the public about Social Security and Medicare issues, and mobilize grassroots efforts to ensure that these programs remain a cornerstone of retirement security for generations to come.

It's like having a vigilant guard at the gate of your financial fortress, protecting your hard-earned benefits from potential threats.

And don't forget about organizations that focus on specific retirement issues, like pension rights or financial literacy. These groups are like specialized units within your retirement army, each tackling a particular challenge and contributing to the overall mission of securing your financial future.

For example, the Pension Rights Center advocates for the protection of pension plans and helps individuals navigate pension-related issues. The National Council on Aging offers programs and resources to enhance the financial security and well-being of older adults.

It's like having a diverse team of experts at your disposal, each providing specialized knowledge and support in their respective areas.

Joining these organizations is not just about receiving benefits and information. It's about becoming an active participant in shaping the future of retirement security.

It's like joining a community of weavers, contributing your thread to the tapestry, and helping to create a more vital and more vibrant artwork.

You can participate in advocacy efforts, write letters to your elected officials, and even volunteer your time to support the organization's mission. It's about making your voice heard and contributing to a collective effort to protect and enhance retirement security for yourself and future generations.

Think of it like joining a chorus of voices, each singing in harmony to create a powerful and resonant message. Together, you can amplify your impact and make a difference in the lives of millions of retirees.

And here's a crucial point: joining organizations that support retirement security is not just for retirees. It's for anyone who cares about the future of retirement and wants to be part of a movement to ensure that everyone has the opportunity to enjoy a secure and fulfilling retirement.

It's like planting seeds for a future harvest, nurturing the growth of a strong and vibrant retirement landscape for generations to come.

By joining these organizations, you're not just advocating for your retirement security; you're becoming part of a more significant movement, a collective effort to create a society where everyone has the opportunity to age with dignity and financial peace of mind.

It's about building a legacy of support, ensuring that the tapestry of retirement security remains strong and vibrant for generations to come.

Chapter 15
Conclusion

15.1 Key Takeaways and Actionable Steps

As we reach the final stretch of our journey together, it's time to gather around the campfire and reflect on the key lessons we've learned along the way. Think of this as our "aha!" moment, where we distill the essence of our exploration and equip you with the tools and knowledge to navigate your retirement path with confidence.

We've trekked through the intricate terrain of Social Security, demystified the COLA calculation, and explored various strategies for maximizing your benefits and securing your financial future. We've also delved into the broader economic landscape, understanding the impact of inflation and the importance of a diversified retirement portfolio.

Now, it's time to pack our backpacks with the most valuable takeaways and actionable steps, ensuring you're well-prepared for the exciting adventure that lies ahead.

First and foremost, remember that **Social Security is a cornerstone of your retirement security**. It's a program you've contributed to throughout your working years, a promise that you'll have a reliable income stream to support you in your golden years.

Think of it as a sturdy base camp, providing a solid foundation for your retirement journey. But it's not the entire expedition. You'll also need other supplies, like savings, investments, and a well-planned route, to reach your desired destination.

Understanding how COLA works is crucial for navigating the ever-changing economic landscape. It's like having a compass that guides you through inflationary storms, ensuring your benefits maintain their purchasing power over time.

Remember that COLA is based on the CPI-W, which measures the average change in prices for a basket of goods and services. While it's not a perfect match for everyone's expenses, it's a vital tool that helps protect your retirement income from erosion.

Claiming Social Security at the right time is like choosing the optimal moment to harvest your crops. Claiming early might provide a smaller yield while delaying can result in a more bountiful harvest.

Consider your circumstances, including your health, financial needs, and family situation, to determine the best claim strategy for you. It's like choosing the right tools for your farming endeavor: ensuring you have the equipment and knowledge to reap the maximum rewards.

Coordinating Social Security with other income sources is like creating a balanced meal. You wouldn't want to eat just one type of food, would you? You'd combine different ingredients to make a nutritious and satisfying diet.

Similarly, in retirement planning, it's essential to have a mix of income sources, including pensions, savings, and investments, to ensure a stable and fulfilling financial life. It's about creating a recipe for economic security, blending different ingredients to achieve a well-rounded and fulfilling retirement.

Protecting your investments from inflation is like safeguarding your crops from pests and diseases. You wouldn't want your hard work to be destroyed by external threats, would you? You'd take preventative measures to protect your harvest and ensure its long-term viability.

Similarly, in retirement planning, it's crucial to protect your investments from the erosive effects of inflation. Diversify your portfolio, consider inflation-protected securities, and stay informed about economic trends to ensure your nest egg remains healthy and vibrant.

Managing healthcare costs in retirement is like tending to your health and well-being. You wouldn't neglect your physical and mental health, would you? You'd prioritize preventive care, seek medical attention when needed, and maintain a healthy lifestyle to ensure a long and fulfilling life.

Similarly, in retirement planning, it's essential to manage healthcare costs proactively. Understand your Medicare options, explore supplemental insurance, and prioritize healthy habits to protect your financial and physical well-being.

Advocating for your retirement security is like being a vigilant guardian of your financial fortress. You wouldn't leave your home unprotected, would you? You'd take measures to secure your property and ensure its safety from potential threats.

Similarly, in retirement planning, it's crucial to advocate for your rights and stay informed about policies that affect your financial security. Join organizations that support retirement security, contact your elected officials, and make your voice heard to protect your hard-earned benefits and ensure a secure future for yourself and future generations.

Now, let's translate these takeaways into actionable steps:
- **Review your Social Security statement regularly.** It's like checking your map to ensure you're on the right track. Make sure your earnings record is accurate and understand your estimated benefits.
- **Estimate your retirement income needs.** It's like calculating the amount of food and supplies you'll need for your journey. Consider your expenses, lifestyle, and potential healthcare costs to determine how much income you'll need in retirement.
- **Develop a retirement savings plan.** It's like packing your backpack with essential provisions for your journey. Set savings goals, explore different investment options, and contribute regularly to your retirement accounts.
- **Consider working with a financial advisor.** It's like having an experienced Sherpa guide you through challenging terrain. A financial advisor can provide personalized advice, help you create a comprehensive plan, and navigate complex financial matters.

- **Stay informed about Social Security and retirement-related issues.** It's like keeping an eye on the weather forecast and adjusting your plans accordingly. Stay updated on COLA changes, legislative developments, and other factors that might affect your retirement security.

By taking these actionable steps, you're equipping yourself with the tools and knowledge to navigate your retirement journey with confidence. It's about being proactive, informed, and adaptable, ready to embrace the challenges and opportunities that lie ahead.

15.2 Building a Fulfilling Retirement Lifestyle

Retirement. That word might conjure up images of lazy days on the beach, endless rounds of golf, or finally tackling that towering stack of books you've been meaning to read. But building a genuinely fulfilling retirement lifestyle goes beyond leisure activities and checking off bucket list items. It's about designing a new chapter in your life, one that's rich with purpose, connection, and joy.

Think of retirement as a blank canvas, a fresh start to paint a masterpiece of your design. You're the artist, and the possibilities are endless. You can choose vibrant colors of adventure, soothing hues of relaxation, or bold strokes of new passions and pursuits.

But just like an artist needs more than just paint and brushes to create a masterpiece, you need more than just time and money to build a fulfilling retirement lifestyle. It's about crafting a life that aligns with your values, interests, and aspirations, a life that brings you a sense of purpose and fulfillment.

One key ingredient in this recipe for a fulfilling retirement is **purpose**. It's like the compass that guides your journey, providing direction and meaning. What gets you excited to wake up in the morning? What makes you feel like you're making a difference?

It could involve volunteering at a local charity, mentoring young people, or sharing your skills and experience with others. It could also include pursuing a long-held passion, like writing a book, learning a new language, or starting a business.

Whatever your purpose, it's about finding something that gives you a sense of meaning and contribution, something that makes you feel like you're making a difference in the world.

Another essential ingredient is **connection**. It's like the glue that holds your retirement tapestry together, weaving together relationships, friendships, and a sense of belonging.

Retirement can be a time to reconnect with old friends, strengthen family bonds, and build new relationships with people who share your interests. Join a book club, volunteer at a community garden, or take a class to meet new people and expand your social circle.

It's about nurturing those connections and creating a support system that enriches your life and provides a sense of belonging.

And don't forget about **joy**. It's like the vibrant colors that bring your retirement canvas to life, adding zest, excitement, and a sense of adventure.

Retirement is a time to pursue your passions, explore new hobbies, and rediscover the things that bring you joy. Travel to new destinations, learn a musical instrument, take up a new sport, or simply spend more time doing the things you love.

It's about embracing life with a sense of curiosity and wonder, finding joy in everyday moments, and creating memories that will last a lifetime.

But, building a fulfilling retirement lifestyle is not just about pursuing your interests. It's also about **giving back to your community**. It's like sharing your harvest with others, contributing to the well-being of your neighborhood and society.

Volunteer your time at a local charity, mentor young people, or get involved in civic engagement. Share your skills and experience with others, leaving a positive impact on the world around you.

It's about paying it forward and contributing to a better future for generations to come.

And here's a crucial point: **building a fulfilling retirement lifestyle is an ongoing process, not a one-time event**. It's like tending to a garden, nurturing your passions, relationships, and well-being over time.

It's about embracing change, adapting to new circumstances, and continuously seeking opportunities for growth and fulfillment. It's about living each day with intention, purpose, and joy.

And remember, retirement is not just about what you do; it's also about who you are. It's about embracing your identity as a retiree, shedding old roles and expectations, and embracing new possibilities.

It's about rediscovering yourself, exploring new facets of your personality, and living authentically. It's about being true to yourself, pursuing your passions, and creating a life that reflects your values and aspirations.

By focusing on purpose, connection, joy, and giving back, you can build a retirement lifestyle that's not just fulfilling but also meaningful and impactful. It's about creating a life that's rich with experiences, relationships, and contributions, a life that leaves a lasting legacy for yourself and those around you.

15.3 Looking Ahead: The Future of Social Security and Retirement

As we reach the final pages of our journey together, it's time to take a deep breath, reflect on the knowledge we've gained, and gaze toward the horizon of what the future holds for Social Security and retirement.

Think of it like reaching the summit of a mountain after a long and challenging climb. You pause to catch your breath, admire the breathtaking view, and contemplate the path that lies ahead.

The future of Social Security and retirement sparks much debate and speculation. It's like peering into a swirling mist, trying to discern the shapes and contours of what lies beyond.

But while there are uncertainties and challenges ahead, there's also reason for optimism and hope. Just like a seasoned explorer who embraces the unknown with a sense of adventure and preparedness, we can approach the future of retirement with a spirit of resilience and adaptability.

One of the critical challenges facing Social Security is its long-term solvency. As we discussed earlier, demographic changes and economic pressures are projected to deplete the program's trust fund in the coming decades.

It's like encountering a fork in the road, where we need to choose a path that ensures the program's sustainability for future generations. This might involve making adjustments to benefit formulas, raising the retirement age, or increasing payroll taxes.

But these changes are not just about numbers and statistics. They're about preserving a promise, a commitment to ensuring that Social Security remains a cornerstone of retirement security for all Americans.

It's like tending to a precious heirloom, carefully preserving it for future generations to cherish and benefit from.

Another challenge is the changing nature of work and retirement. The traditional model of a lifelong career followed by a clear-cut pension is becoming less common. People are working longer, changing jobs more frequently, and pursuing a variety of paths in their later years.

That presents both challenges and opportunities for Social Security and retirement planning. It's like navigating a new terrain, where the old maps might not be entirely accurate, and we need to adapt our strategies to reach our destination.

One opportunity is the growing awareness of the importance of retirement planning. More and more people are recognizing that Social Security alone might not be enough to provide a comfortable retirement, and they're taking proactive steps to save and invest for their future.

It's like packing extra provisions for your journey, ensuring you have the resources to sustain you along the way.

Another opportunity is the rise of technology and innovation. From online retirement calculators to personalized financial advice apps, technology is empowering individuals to take control of their retirement planning and make informed decisions.

It's like having a high-tech compass that guides you through the retirement landscape, providing real-time information and personalized recommendations.

And don't forget about the power of community and advocacy. By joining organizations that support retirement security, staying informed about policy changes, and making your voice heard, you can contribute to a collective effort to shape the future of retirement for yourself and future generations.

It's like joining a caravan of fellow travelers, sharing knowledge, supporting each other, and advocating for a smoother and more accessible path for all.

As we look ahead, it's important to remember that retirement is not just about finances. It's about living a fulfilling life, pursuing your passions, and contributing to your community.

It's like reaching the summit and realizing that the journey itself was just as rewarding as the destination.

Whether you envision a retirement filled with travel, hobbies, volunteering, or simply spending time with loved ones, it's crucial to plan for a lifestyle that aligns with your values and aspirations.

It's like painting a masterpiece of your retirement years, using your unique palette of experiences, talents, and dreams to create a vibrant and fulfilling canvas.

And remember, retirement is not an endpoint; it's a new beginning, a chapter filled with opportunities for growth, exploration, and connection. It's a time to embrace new challenges, discover hidden passions, and leave your mark on the world.

So, as you embark on this exciting new chapter, remember the lessons we've learned together, stay informed, be adaptable, and most importantly, embrace the journey with a sense of adventure and optimism.

The future of Social Security and retirement might be uncertain. Still, with careful planning, a resilient spirit, and a supportive community, you can navigate the path ahead with confidence and create a retirement that is both financially secure and personally fulfilling.

www.ingramcontent.com/pod-product-compliance
Lightning Source LLC
Chambersburg PA
CBHW052151220526
45471CB00004B/1632